Ten years after paying off their first hou
and having bought and paid off two in
the meantime—Anita Bell now lives n
land, with her husband, Jim, their two
menagerie in the family's new dream home. Anita is an energetic full-time mother and independent businesswoman (Jim
notes that she has one employee: him). She is working on
numerous projects, including her first novel, *Crystal Coffin*, and
she relaxes by painting, doing leatherwork and other craft
projects, fishing, and riding her horses. Her first book *Your
Mortgage and How to Pay it off in Five Years by someone who did it in
three* was the bestselling Australian non-fiction book of 1999.

YOUR MONEY
STARTING OUT AND STARTING OVER

ANITA BELL

RANDOM HOUSE AUSTRALIA

Published by Random House Australia Pty Ltd
Level 3, 100 Pacific Highway, North Sydney, NSW 2060
http://www.randomhouse.com.au

Sydney New York Toronto
London Auckland Johannesburg
and agencies throughout the world

First published in 2001

National Library of Australia
Cataloguing-in-Publication Data

Bell, Anita, 1967–.
    Your money: starting out and starting over.

ISBN 978 1 74051 089 9.
ISBN 1 74051 089 5.

1. Investments. 2. Finance, Personal. I. Title.

332.024

Typeset by Midland Typesetters, Victoria
Printed and bound by Griffin Press, South Australia

Illustration on page 236 copied and modified under licence from
T/Maker Company.

20 19 18

Contents

Acknowledgements

This book is dedicated to those thousands of readers who stopped me in the street to thank me for the first one and ask for more, and to my wonderful family who supported me in the process.

Introduction

Hand anyone a fast $5000, and they'll easily plan a holiday or a party or a makeover for the old homestead. But give them an annual salary of $15,000–$50,000 and they'll usually be stumped when it comes to planning a budget to take care of that much money over that long a period.

Money slips through our fingers—too easily. Case studies later show how some people waste as much as 70% of their net income without realising it.

But it doesn't have to be this way. There's stacks you can do to make your finances more bearable, no matter what level of income you're blessed or cursed with. From clean slates to financial disasters, whether you're 15 or 50, starting out or starting over, the following pages are jam-packed with hints, tips and tricks on nearly every aspect of your money.

This book contains the lessons that I had to learn the hard way—so you don't. Right, let's start getting your financial life into shape then you can concentrate on getting everything you want out of the rest of your life.

ANITA BELL'S
DEFINITION OF FINANCIAL SUCCESS

Living every day, debt-free (or with negatively geared
investments which greatly exceed your debt)

Working by choice, without having to worry about
job security

Doing the things you like, whenever you like, but still
respecting your responsibilities

Having cash in your pocket and having friends and
family to share it with

… no matter how small your income or the kind of
job you have.

1

Reprogram for Success

ARE YOU PROGRAMMED TO FAIL?

Too often, what we hear the loudest in the news is the dire warnings about the economy: soaring unemployment, inflation, the falling value of the Aussie peso, and high interest rates. For me, this was particularly annoying in my last years of high school. At a time when I needed to concentrate on getting the best grades I could manage, I was bombarded with the concept that there were no jobs out there for any of us and we were all going to fail. I've never been very good at concentrating on more than one thing at a time, so I ignored the bad news, deciding there wasn't much I could do about it for now—so why worry?

When the time came for me to get thrown out into the real world I pulled my head out of the sand and took a look around. I saw two things. First, that my science-based education—although amongst the best in the southern hemisphere—left me standing naked of financial skills in a world that revolved around money. And second, that despite the dire predictions, a fair percentage of people were still driving around in nice cars, living in nice homes and smiling as they passed me in the street—and many of these people seemed like ordinary folks, just like me.

This gave me hope. All I had to do—I innocently thought—was figure out what they were doing and follow the crowd.

Boy, was I wrong. Honestly, it's as if someone stamps the word *sucker* on your forehead the moment you earn your first pay cheque. I learned some very hard lessons very quickly. So I stepped back and re-evaluated before I let myself get into too much trouble.

What did these people have, I asked myself, that I wanted? And the answer was obvious: income, wheels and property. So these became my first three goals, all of which I achieved in my first three months out of high school.

Admittedly, I started at the lowest end of the scale. My income came firstly as unemployment cheques, then from a supermarket chain where I became a casual shop attendant at the very bottom of the pecking order. My car had almost as much experience on the road as I had of breathing outside my mother's belly, and my property was only vacant land. But I was happy. Technically speaking, I had achieved what I had set out to achieve before many of my friends had even handed in their first assignments at university.

Yes, I was studying too, but I was doing it at a slower pace by correspondence. And yes, I did sign a contract to buy the land and have to defer settlement until after my seventeenth birthday, but this saw the last of my three major goals achieved long before I'd even earned my open driver's licence. (And one last yes—during this period I was paying board to my parents too—at about the same rate as some people were paying in rent.) So I got excited—very excited.

You don't have to be rich to have fun with money.

This money thing didn't seem so difficult after all and I had the rest of my life to get better at it. So I looked to the next step: paying off the land and upgrading each of my goals to the next level: improving the job, improving the car, improving the property.

That's where everything started to get complicated, but it's where I learned most of my best lessons; things I later used to help many of my friends and family to catch up.

You can use these hints, tips and tricks too. All you have to do before you start is ask yourself: have you been programmed to fail? Do you feel defeated when you hear that jobs are scarce, prices are rising and interest rates are soaring? Or do you smile and do something about it?

The difference comes down to a simple choice—and that choice is all yours to make.

On the subject of poo-pooers

When striving to achieve something against the crowd, it always helps me to remember some of the great clangers of all time:

- *Who the hell wants to hear actors talk?*—said H.M. Warner, founder of Warner Brothers (silent pictures), in 1927.
- *I think there is a world market for maybe five computers,* said Thomas Watson, chairman of IBM in 1943.
- *Guitar music is on the way out,* said Decca Recording Co when they rejected the Beatles in 1962.

And my personal favourite . . .

- *640K* [of computer memory] *ought to be enough for anybody,* said THE Bill Gates in 1981.

Okay—if you're ready—let's take one step closer to the fun. First you need to figure out which financial category you fit into.

Who are you?

SINK = Single Income person with No Kids, living at home or renting.

DINK = Double Income couple, with No Kids, renting or with a long mortgage. If you're paying your house off in five years or less—or if your current mortgage owing is over $150,000—then consider yourself the equivalent of a single income family, for the purposes of this book.

Single Income Family = two parents with one income and also includes single parents living on a pension with or without child support from their ex.

Double Income Family is where both people in the couple receive income, even if that income is only a pension. If the double income is earned by only one person who works two jobs, then tax disadvantages mean you'll be better off considering yourself as a single income family for the purposes of this book.

2

Financial Achievements—
A Goal Guide and Problem Solver
for Every Age

Everyone is different. And everyone has different ideas about what they want to do and how. I don't want to curb individualism in the slightest. I'm not going to tell you what you have to do and when you have to do it. What I do want to show is what your options *really can be*.

I want to show you how to work out for yourself what you want and when, and then how to work out how to get it, no matter how much you earn, where you live, or what you want out of life.

To do this, I've put together years worth of my number-crunching for friends and come up with a goal guide that either suits, or can be easily adapted by, practically every Aussie who's competent to open their own wallet.

For the pedantics out there, this is NOT a guarantee of what you'll get if you follow this plan. As much as I'd enjoy the prospect, I won't be around to whack you over the head with this book every time you let your budget blow. (Bulges aren't so bad by the way, it's the total blow-outs that hurt.)

Instead, use this chapter in two ways:
- As a guide to what is easily possible when you start fresh out of high school with a clean slate.
- As a guide to help you start over, when you wake up to

find yourself buried in debt doodoo and you want to climb out and catch up on the things you've missed out on.

This chapter is about helping you decide what it is in life that you really want—and roughly when. The rest of the book will help you achieve everything you choose via the express-lane, warning you of the traps and filling you in on the tricks.

You CAN fix your financial mistakes starting today. You CAN get your finances sorted out—easily and quickly. And you CAN catch yourself up without winning lotto.

It's *never* too late to catch up. You can make things financially easier for yourself—at any stage—effective for every single pay. If you doubt this for a second, skip straight to the Radical Case Studies chapter in this book and see what a difference only a handful of tips have made for each of these real people who had real problems.

Start today and make every single paypacket a reason to celebrate.

Warning: Some of the goals I'm about to suggest may seem impossible on a low income. I've learned to expect that criticism. I never did convince some of my friends—even when they were standing on my land with the bank statements in their hands—that I'd paid off my first block by my eighteenth birthday. But I assure you that these goals are easily attainable. They are the goals that I set for myself and that I helped others to set in order to catch up.

Because I'm the kind of person who likes to plan for delays so the overall goal is never compromised, these goals are actually quite conservative. To see how I blew them away much earlier, I've included a section How I Cheated Time immediately afterwards. It's not comprehensive. There are so many things you can do with careful planning that I could never fit them all into one book—and some of the best and most radical ideas are in later chapters.

Right now, I just want to open your eyes to the possibilities—

and the biggest dangers—because once you have the idea, there will be no stopping you.

AGES 15 to 20

This is your chance to get streets ahead of everyone else. Now's the best time to establish your work wardrobe, start your working career, do extra study, get a car, furniture and a deposit for property. Yes, travel is an option now too, especially before you leave school.

Most importantly, it's the best time to learn financial discipline and flexibility. For example, if you really need a car and can pay it off quickly—or if you can pay cash for it—by delaying your furniture collection or travel, then do that. Avoid paying interest on anything as long as you can.

That's not to say you can't have a credit card; quite the opposite. Use hints from chapter 8 to turn your credit card into the hardest working slave you'll ever have.

Biggest opportunities at this stage are in converting your money into useful assets and not letting your age or lack of experience be a barrier to getting the things you want.

Biggest traps are in dining out regularly with friends, borrowing to travel overseas, getting ripped off buying a car, failing to plan, failing to get a good credit rating and failing to budget.

Your 18th birthday

Congratulations, it's now compulsory for you to vote.

As soon as you turn 18, nip into your nearest post office and enrol to vote in federal, state and local elections, or face possible prosecution the next time the rolls are checked in association with an election.

(If you're unemployed your Centrelink payments are called Youth Allowance at this stage. After 21, you get Newstart Allowance. (See also Appendix VI: Pennies from Heaven.)

Tip for the last day of school: While all your friends are brain-dead from exams and raging off to the coast for major R&R, ring 13 24 90 and register for Youth Allowance. The sooner you apply, the sooner you get paid. For more information see Appendix VI, Pennies from Heaven, or check out Centrelink's website at www.centrelink.gov.au.

Tip for your 17th birthday: Ring the Australian Tax Office (ATO) on 13 28 63 and ask for an application form for a Tax File Number (TFN) to be sent to you. You need to supply a tax file number to every employer and financial institution you ever have after you turn 17 so they take out the normal rate of tax instead of a whopping 48.5%. Save yourself a LOT of hassle by applying for a TFN right away. It stays with you for life, it doesn't oblige you to do anything, and it certainly makes life cheaper in the short term, by saving you from having too much tax deducted.

More hints which are great for this age group, but apply to anyone are:

WORK WARDROBE

Goal: To buy anything you need to hit the interview trail—if you don't have it already—by the end of the first week after your final exams.

That's a minimum of two 'as new' job interview outfits which are comfortable and don't make you sweat. (If you're going to be terrified, you might as well be comfy.) You also need at least five casual sets of clothes suitable for the broadest range of jobs that you're interested in—until you get a job with a special uniform, your everyday clothes will usually do. Don't sink cash into uniforms before the job is yours—you'll feel strange and out-of-pocket wearing steel-capped safety boots at a hair salon.

How to get it: Ask friends and family for clothes or clothes' vouchers for birthdays, Easter and Christmas in your last two years at school. (Vouchers from either the Coles Myer or Woolworths chains give you a broad range of shops to choose from.) If you're buying an outfit for graduation night, make sure it's something you can also wear to an interview—or adjust so it's suitable. Save up and buy clothes in end of season sales. And trade extra chores around the house for extra cash or cheaper board from your parents. Or tidy yards or homes for elderly neighbours—many retired ladies can adjust old clothes from St Vinnie's to look modern and new again.

A STEADY JOB

Goal: Within 12 months. It doesn't matter if it's full-time work sweeping up chook poo at an egg farm or part-time work hacking cancers off people's backsides with a laser—just so long as it pays more than what you get on social security, is bearable to show up to at least three days out of five, and is permanent enough to give you six months or more at a time with which to forecast your budget.

How to get it: Be mentally prepared to take the full 12 months to achieve your goal and be prepared to do part-time or casual work in the meantime. Be confident. Know that you will be successful. Be prepared to do anything (anything legal that is!). **Don't wait for jobs to be advertised.** Seek them out yourself, even if you're registered with up to five job network providers (employment agencies that are free because they're government funded). Visit local businesses and ask to be put on their waiting lists, or ask them if you can put up a notice that you're looking for work near where their customers wait for service. And ask them to keep you in mind if their other business contacts get vacancies. **Start job searching BEFORE you leave school (or your current job).** Don't give yourself December as a holiday after graduation. Get ahead of the competition by applying before you cram for exams. Make a list of possible employers, starting with chainstores that offer staff discounts. (Then, use your discounts to trade for cheaper board with your parents.) **Don't be choosy.** You can still keep your eye open for your 'ideal' job while you're working.

A RELIABLE CAR
Goal: Deposit saved in your first six months of working—or in time to apply for your learner's permit. Car—if required—purchased within 12 months.

How to get it: Work part-time after school or on weekends as soon as you turn 15. If you want to get trade skills as well as money, apply for a 'new apprenticeship' to do *during* school hours or a traineeship for after hours. On the way home from your last day at school, drop in your application for Youth Allowance at your local Centrelink—even if you're working part-time. You can't drop it in before you leave school, but there's nothing stopping you from filling in the form ready for your last school day.

See chapter 10 for how to get the best value car for your money.

Never envy a friend who's been given a car by their parents until you've seen the leash they have to wear when they drive it.

EXTRA QUALIFICATIONS
Goal: To get the qualifications you want to take you as far as possible. This could be a university degree or diploma, a trade, or even just a certificate in personal skills development through TAFE. The advantages to doing it now are that you're used to studying, everything's fresh in your mind AND you get the financial benefit of having your chosen qualifications for the longest portion of your working career.

Don't sweat if you don't know what you want to do yet. Many university courses—like Bachelor of Business for example—will take you a long way in a wide choice of careers. If you change your mind during the course, you can often switch and apply for credit for the studies you've completed if they're also applicable to the new course.

And yes, it can be harder to get back into it when you're older because of work, family and motivation challenges—but it's not impossible.

How to get it: If your parents had an education fund for you, use it to pay your HECS payments up front until it runs out. If they didn't put aside savings—or if the money has run out—ask if they'll make up the difference between what you can afford to pay and what the subjects actually cost, in exchange for extra chores or work in their family business.

Birthdays add an extra possibility. Instead of gift certificates from relatives, ask for a cheque made out to the Australian Tax Office and post it to the ATO, Locked bag 1793, Penrith NSW, 1793 with a covering letter telling them your tax file number and advising them that the cheque attached is an EXTRA payment for HECS. Type up a standard letter and give it to your rellies to make it easier for them to send the cheque.

Manipulate your earnings if you're close to the top of one of the income brackets used for calculating your HECS debt. For example, if you're a casual employee and have earned $12,984.00 and you've been offered one more hour's work for the financial year, you might want to turn it down, as it will make the difference between paying $660 HECS that year or not. *Note*: You're not avoiding HECS, merely delaying it until you can afford it. See Tax Pack, the ATO or your accountant for income brackets.

Buy textbooks secondhand through the student union or uni bookshop. Team up with a friend or two and take the same subjects but in different semesters, so you can share textbooks. At the end of the year, sell the books and start again with the next set of subjects. Buy them again once you're a professional and they'll be tax deductible.

GLORY FURNITURE (AGES 12... YES 12... TO 20.)

Goal: To own your own bed and a storage cabinet full of household goods by the time you're 18.

Note: Your grandmother would have called this a glory box, but try starting with a wall unit or wardrobe—it fits more in and is more functional. It was previously a girl thing, but guys are wise to do it now too. Use it to store a collection of setting-up-house essentials: basic handyperson tools like a battery-operated drill and a hammer, linen, cutlery, an iron, kettle, saucepans and toilet paper. Then collect other furniture. Suggestions include: one or two wall units, a trunk or wardrobe for storage, your bedroom suite, a TV, washing machine and refrigerator, or a savings account so you're ready to purchase them.

Sounds weird, I know, to be collecting furniture before you leave high school, but you're going to leave home eventually. The sooner you start stocking up, the easier you make it on yourself later on. You also get the bonus sense of responsibility because you're contributing to the comfort of your family—if you share your belongings, that is. The only real challenge is finding room for everything until you move out, so try buying furniture that your family can use in the meantime like coffee tables, TV and a sewing machine.

How to get it: Buy a storage wardrobe or wall unit cheaply secondhand from a shop or garage sale. Buy one thing to put in it at least every second pay, starting with little things and the basics. Start from as young as 12 if you can, asking for and storing useful presents instead of using them. If you're living at home, trade extra chores so you can keep your own bed if nothing else when you move out.

> **Hint: If you're living at home, make your first storage unit a big empty one, because nature—abhorring a vacuum—invented mothers to help you fill it.**

Note: Mothers (and grandmothers) are notorious nesters.

Since their own nest is usually fully feathered by the time you're about to fly, they'll often make regular contributions if they see something they can't resist buying for you when they're out. Let them. It's good for their sanity and great for your wallet.

SOUND SYSTEM, SPORTING EQUIPMENT OR EXPENSIVE HOBBY SUPPLIES

Goal: One big personal expense to celebrate your first job. The choice is totally up to you, but for many people it often involves either a serious sound system, a personal TV, a video recorder or expensive clothes like a leather jacket—for me, it was a new saddle.

How to get it: Decide what you want, shop around, and save up for it. (See also chapter 4: Lazy Budgeting that Does Everything Except the Dishes and chapter 14: Smart Shopping: Save Money while you Spend.)

Warning 1: Avoid blowing your first six pays from any new job on personal luxuries. It corrodes your discipline and undermines good spending habits. Instead, treat personal luxuries as if they are rewards for a particular effort—eg. a TV as reward for keeping your new job for three months. Never buy a personal luxury until *after* your living expenses are under control and your current bills have been paid.

Warning 2: Avoid putting luxuries on credit or layby if you can't pay them off in two or three pays. Doing so is an admission that you can't afford them yet, that you haven't earned enough money to deserve them yet, and that you have more important expenses to cope with first.

CREDIT RATING

Goal: To establish a credit rating *before* you need it. Whenever you apply for a loan or a bill account with a major company or organisation—like phone or power companies—your application has a much higher chance of approval if you have a good credit rating. If you don't have a good credit rating, you may be forced to get loans from finance companies with ravenous fees and interest rates if you do need to borrow money.

How to get it: Never make a late payment for anything, including your rent. As soon as you turn 18, apply for a credit card which has a 55-day interest-free period. Then operate it like a bill savings account, buying small things often and paying them off often—preferably out of the paypacket that you earn the same week or fortnight as you make the purchase.

Trick: You don't ever have to go into the red on your credit card account if you don't want to. You can deposit the money into your credit card just like depositing to a savings account—technically making it overpaid—and use the credit card (which has no EFTPOS fees) to withdraw the money when you pay for things.

OVERSEAS TRAVEL

Goal: To travel to at least one overseas country. (Only if you want to. Don't bow to peer pressure!)

How to get it: This age group can take advantage of youth exchange programs before leaving high school or university, making most flights cheap and most accommodation free. Likewise, if you get your family to host a foreign student rather than actually going overseas yourself, you may be able to visit that student in following years without paying accommodation (or tour guide fees).

Warning: Lengthy periods overseas not only cost you the money you have saved up to spend on them, they also cost you the income you could have been earning if you didn't go away. Always work out both of these amounts, and weigh them against the other things you want in life before planning your financial goals to success. You may not have to give anything up; you might just have to work harder and shuffle your priorities to stay on track.

DEPOSIT FOR PROPERTY

Goal: $1000 minimum a year in savings for a house or land. *That's only $20 a week.*

If you're hoping to get hitched in your early twenties, double this or encourage your partner to match your savings as soon as possible. Try to resist using shared bank accounts until *after* you've been living together for more than a year—because money arguments turn love into resentment very quickly.

How to get it: At this stage—unless you're *really* keen like me—you're just being far-sighted, so you only need to save slowly. If you need to buy property unexpectedly—or if a great deal crops up—check out chapter 16: The Fast $5000 Rescue Package.

Don't let your age be an excuse not to buy property. I signed my first contract to buy land a few weeks before I turned 17. To get around the legal problems of being underage, settlement was extended to after my birthday and my parents agreed to be guarantors.

Beware of fairytales: Even in the planning stages, you'll hear things that might put you off buying property, like *you can't afford to buy in this area.* Salespeople may try to convince you there are no homes for sale in the suburbs you're after. What they're really saying is that they have no listings in that area, so they'll try to sell you somewhere else—and they'll often start with the properties that haven't been selling.

Don't be fooled. No matter where you buy, you have to be happy with the area. (Yes, even if it's an investment property you're buying, because if you wouldn't live there, you can't expect to get good tenants to want to live there either.) It's going to be your little island of sanity after a hard day at work. Coming home from work should feel like a holiday every afternoon.

Your biggest advantage in starting to look around early is to keep your eyes open for opportunities like deceased estates. Keep your eye on the garage sales where housefuls of furniture are being sold for clues to properties that might be coming up.

Your other big advantage in planning early, is in giving you time to find a good friend or relative who is also interested in buying a house or flat. DO NOT SHARE THE PURCHASE OF ONE PROPERTY. That's inviting financial wars like you've never known before.

Instead, work towards buying yourselves property to rent to each other. That way, you're almost guaranteed to have good tenants, you can negotiate your rents to be mutually affordable, and you get to negative-gear your own home for a few years until you decide to swap and move in (or whatever).

The only downside is you don't get the $7000 First Home Owner Grant for investment properties and stamp duty can be higher. But tax and low rent benefits can make up for this fairly promptly.

EXTRA WARNING: Beware of the valuations of house/land packages with low or no deposits— especially if lending is arranged for you with the developer's preferred lender. Make sure you get an independent valuation to ensure the place is worth what you're told it is, because too many buyers wake up after a few years to discover they owe far more than the property was ever worth.

AGES 21 to 30

Okay, you've finished your degree—if you wanted one—and you've found yourself a reliable job, which hopefully you enjoy. If you've been doing full-time study, you may also want to do some 'living' to catch up—although you'll also have some major income to catch up on too. People who finished at Year 12 might already be at least $120,000 ahead of you.

Regardless of your education, you're often turning your thoughts to accumulating assets, a house, getting your investment portfolio under way, upgrading to a nice car and maybe planning a family to fill the back seats.

But you don't have to fully settle down just yet. Your feet might still be itchy for travel or you might want to set your sights a little higher up the career ladder first.

If you've been blowing your money so far, then now's the best time to end your naughty ways. You can fix your budget and set yourself up for life either before your youngsters come along, or before they're old enough to worry about what brand of joggers they're wearing. Yes, babies are the cheapest to keep—especially when they're breastfed. So now's also the best time to establish neighbourly or family networks for hand-me-downs.

Biggest opportunities are in the $7000 First Home Owner Grant, in getting debt-free before children arrive (or at least before they start preschool), and in being a little strict with yourself now to set up an enviable asset base to last forever.

Biggest traps are in getting ripped off buying house and land packages, trading up your car every two or three years, committing financially to relationships before you're emotionally ready, going away on holidays that you can't afford, keeping your credit card fully in debt, planning big families that you can't support without government assistance, borrowing to buy furniture, failing to plan your children's next ten years, getting caught for running small businesses from home without declaring the income for tax and failing to budget.

(If you're unemployed your Centrelink payments are called

Newstart Allowance (after 21) with different entitlements to Youth Allowance. See also Appendix VI: Pennies from Heaven or contact Centrelink.)

MARRIAGE
No, you don't have to get married as such. I include de facto relationships in this too. *After* you have a fair idea that you can put up with your partner's toenail clippings and other disgusting habits—which could take up to a year by itself—I suggest:

Goal 1: Completing a 12-month (minimum) financial 'apprenticeship' together, watching and learning how your possible partner handles money—setting joint goals, but keeping savings accounts and big purchases safely separate in case you split up. You don't have to live together to start this apprenticeship, but you do need to spend a few hours with each other every day. Also use this time to get to know your partner thoroughly. Plan activities where you work together under stress— like building something for your parents-in-law-to-be, or repairing the car together, or setting up a tent and camping for a few days without shopping regularly for top-up supplies. If you're going to live as man and wife, you have to be able to work as a team in all things, not only money management.

Goal 2: Six months to one year—in addition to your apprenticeship—to plan and save for a wedding, honeymoon and your deposit for a house. You don't have to be living together during your financial apprenticeship, but a few weeks' holiday together at least certainly helps you to figure out your spending and saving strengths and weaknesses together.

How to get it: Your honeymoon is your chance to kill two budget birds with one stone: to scratch those itchy travel feet and to celebrate your start to wedded bliss. Make sure you both agree on the destination and avoid getting into debt to pay for either your wedding or your honeymoon. Also see chapter 17: Radical Case Studies, Case Study 3: Wedding Bells and chapter 14 for hints and tricks about saving money along the way.

$5000–$10,000 DEPOSIT FOR PROPERTY

Goal: To save or acquire this within 12 to 24 months. Yes, you will need to aim higher if you want to buy a place in one of the popular areas of most capital cities. But remember that some lenders require only 5% deposit—usually, but not always, excluding the $7000 First Home Owner Grant—($14,000, if you're building) so it may not be as big a goal as you think.

How to get it: A small portion must be saved regularly—the bank will be looking at this to judge your reliability and commitment upon application for a home loan. Deposits to managed funds or shares also count.

If you have a very solid relationship with your partner, moving in together to combine transport, accommodation and living costs can give you extra savings to bank, but do it in a way that makes it obvious to an outsider who owns what—just in case the relationship breaks down.

Also negotiate down the price of the property as far as possible, since the lower the purchase price, the lower your deposit needs to be. Yes, you also need a few extra thousand for legal fees and stamp duties and you're still aiming to get the biggest, fattest deposit possible to save you thousands in interest in the long run, so regardless of where you want to live, check out chapter 16, the Fast $5000 Rescue Package for radical hints on how to get big bucks fast for deposits.

BUYING A HOUSE

Goal: From 3 to 8 years, depending on whether you've got kids or not. Now's your best chance to buy and pay off a house quickly—with two incomes and with young or no children.

How to get it: As mentioned earlier, consider looking for a friend or relative who wishes to buy a house—as you do—but can't quite afford it. Don't share the purchase of one house if you can avoid it, as relationship problems and different long-term goals can ruin everything. Consider instead buying houses to rent to each other so you can both negative-gear. Naturally you'll have to live in each other's houses, but you at least know your tenants will look after the place—or else! This also makes ownership faster and cheaper—since the Tax Office makes major contributions to your repayments. If the relationship sours, or maybe if one of you wishes to sell up and go elsewhere, at least the other person still has a house that is theirs, they just have to move into it.

OR . . .

As a rough guide, manipulate your deposit and the purchase price so the loan is equal to about twice your annual income (single income if you're single or combined income if you're a couple), and so that it's practically a breeze to pay it off in five years or less. (You'll already know all the tricks that help with this, because no doubt you've already read my previous book!)

BASIC FURNITURE FOR EVERY ROOM
Goal: 18 months. Prioritise what you need according to your lifestyle and whether you're renting or mortgaged—start with a fridge, washing machine, bed(s), TV, lounge, dining suite and improvise with everything else until you can pay cash. For example, you don't need an ironing board if you've got a kitchen bench you can put a towel over; you don't need a dining suite if you've got a breakfast bar and you rarely have guests over etc.

How to get it: It rarely makes financial sense to rent it if you can buy it (or make do until you can buy it). Renting fridges, dishwashers and many other major appliances can eventuate into very expensive little loans if you miss any repayments. Please remember, if you can't afford it NOW, you can't have it, or else you're robbing your own future. See chapter 4 for tips on budgeting and then getting the best value for your buck.

SET UP YOUR OWN BUSINESS
Goal: To construct or buy a business to run as an owner–operator. Set-up time, maximum two months. The choice is yours. There's stacks to choose from. Go it alone with your own trade or idea, or buy an established business or franchise

through a business broker or business-for-sale style magazine from your newsagent.

How to get it: Forecast everything on a worse-case scenario and figure out a way to survive operating like this for up to 18 months. Write out a business plan with costings, stages in which you expect to build the company, goals you want the company to achieve and product and advertising strategies you want to use. Choose an accountant who has other clients with similar businesses and make an appointment to go through your business plan and organise company registration and strategies to minimise tax including personally run superannuation funds if desired. Contact the Australian Tax Office on 13 24 78 and organise an ABN and GST registration information to be sent to you so you can choose—with your accountant's advice—which way you want or have to go for GST: registered or unregistered. And as an alternative to bank finance, ring the Australian Stock Exchange on 1300 300 279 and ask for information on their enterprise market, which is how they can help you find investors for new ventures which are too small to list on the stock exchange. Be very cautious of lenders who charge outrageous interest rates for business. (This list is only the basics. See your accountant for more info.)

How NOT to get it: By putting a second mortgage on your home. If your business is likely to be profitable, you shouldn't have trouble getting finance for it on its own.

If your proposed company is not likely to be profitable, you should think twice before starting it anyway and you certainly shouldn't be risking your house on it, especially if you have kids.

CHILDREN

Goal: You're on your own with this one, but I suggest nothing under 12 months if you can help it. (That's how long it takes for the tablet to wear off and the bun to cook properly.)

How to get them: Hmmm, let's stick to the money side of things shall we? Mothers are legally required to take at least six weeks off work after birth. But you can take off up to a year without pay in most jobs without risking your employment if you've been working for that employer for 12 months. Some industrial awards also offer a portion of your maternity leave on full pay or allow you to take your holidays or long-service leave as part of your time off. So ask your pay office about your entitlements *before* planning bumpkins. (See case study 2.)

Work out how long you want off—assuming baby is healthy—and time your absence without pay to fall equally over the end of one financial year and into the next one. That way—in addition to a baby—you'll give birth to two healthy tax return cheques in a row. (That's because tax is deducted on the assumption that you're going to earn the same amount all year. If you stop working earlier, your tax often works out to be overpaid.) Of course, you are then dependent on nature to play along with your plans, but it doesn't hurt to try it this way.

Take out comprehensive heath insurance *before* you discover the hole in your condom. Choosing a private ward in a public hospital if you can will save you big bucks in 'gap' fees that you often get if you go through a private hospital. Make sure you have family cover, because the baby may not be covered (or even considered to be a patient, for that matter!) Also, some health funds have only small gaps in cover with some hospitals and big gaps with others, so ask your hospital or health fund about gaps before joining.

Once you have had the baby, apply for all family allowances and entitlements from Centrelink *before* leaving hospital because late applications may not be backdated to the baby's date of birth. The nurse or social worker should supply these forms for you.

Check out Case Study 2: The Expectant Couple for more tips.

If bumpkins is premmie, buy new dolls' clothes of the cabbage-patch variety cheap from flea markets. They're perfect for tykes smaller than size 000.

AGES 31 to 40

By this stage, most people have kids, either in nappies or with double-digit ages. They've also got mortgages, car loans and credit cards. And if you're in a mess, you're usually in a *big* mess. But it's been my experience that it's still easy to fix.

This is the best time to teach your kids by example that money management can be easy, fun and worthwhile. Learn to set goals as a family and your children will become keen to participate by using rewards for them, just as you use rewards for yourself. When you fill your first inground pool, or take your first luxury family car for a burn, they'll appreciate it for what it is—a reward for working together to achieve success.

Plan *now* for your children's university education and first car—if that's what you'd like to do—to make it easiest for you in the long run. The longer you leave it, the harder these costs will hit you when the time comes, emotionally as well as financially. You don't have to pay for everything and you don't have to tell them you're putting money away—it's good for them to budget so they're paying too, but it's great to be able to surprise them with the bonus. It's a last big helping hand into the real world. Don't underestimate how giving this with no strings attached can make you feel as a parent, as well as what it can do for your children.

Biggest advantages include being able to refine your definition of what you want in life, being young enough, but wise enough to appreciate the rewards for your efforts, and being young enough to enjoy it with your family. You also have the advantage of the mistakes you've made so far—you can avoid making them again and you can teach others, so you turn bad experiences into good.

Biggest traps: Divorce (including ongoing child support, splitting up assets—often at a loss, having to start from scratch and inability to afford to start another family); getting ripped off buying investment homes or conned into starting savings plans that have big operating and exit fees that devour your returns; and refinancing your home loan to buy a new car and not making extra repayments, so you end up paying off the car over ten years or more.

Goal: Within 3 to 5 years. *Either* have an investment property paid off and the next one started; *or* other shares or investments totalling more than $100,000 (net); *or* upgrade home, cars and furniture using mostly cash AND have a minimum of $40,000 in other investments.

Yes, you can upgrade home, cars and furniture to luxury versions now if you've been good little budgeters, because you won't have to get very deep into debt to do it—$20,000 to $100,000 is usually enough, depending on how big a makeover you're going for, even if you've got kids and you've had to drop to one wage for a few years. Remember you should have a debt-free home behind you now, as well as considerable assets that you can use to spoil yourself a little if you wish—you should be able to afford it by now.

If not, let's fix it. If you're 31 now, you've got 10 years to the next age bracket, giving you heaps more time than you need to clear your debts and start saving for the future. That's a piece of cake—particularly on two incomes—and especially if your kids are old enough to get part-time jobs and help support themselves. That way the costs of raising your kids can drop to roughly the equivalent of having two nappy-wearing breastfed babies for every teenager. (Don't tell them that, or they'll probably freak!)

Grab the opportunity now to overhaul your budget and hit your debts hard to catch up, and the rewards will be that you'll have up to 15 years of comfortable debt-free living to enjoy life and save up before your retirement.

How to get it: Make sure your upgrades to your car, home and furniture will last and make you happy for another ten to 20 years. That shouldn't be a problem when buying quality this time round.

Now's also the time to think about setting up a company to manage your investments and your own superannuation fund—even if you're not self-employed or run a business—because there are generous tax benefits and various loopholes for sheltering your assets from legal and inflation dangers by doing this. (See your accountant and chapter 12 for details).

AGES 41 to 50

If you've been bad: Financial nightmares can still be repaired. Debts can still be cleared—often with renewed vigour if kids have moved out or if they're fully supporting themselves at home. Your problems can still be fixed and your bad spending habits can still be changed—but you *are* getting close to your last chance to clear your debts and get finances under control with enough time to live it up before retirement. (Not that living stops at retirement!) You don't usually have to retire until 65, so you can still have a safety net of up to 15 years, but you don't want to waste this time, or you'll be dependent on welfare and family until you eventually cark it.

If you've been good, or caught up: Then you're on target. You're debt-free. And your investments are growing by themselves, so growth combined with top-ups of around $30,000 to $60,000 a year should be an easy target. Early retirement or cutting down your working hours should also be an option now.

Likely outlays: You may have your kids' weddings to help pay for. (Don't be old-fashioned—if you've only got sons, pitch in just as hard for their wedding as if they were daughters you were forking out for). And this doesn't have to be limited to the traditional contribution to grog and the honeymoon. You might like to kick in a cheque for their house deposit, three months worth of repayments, or the legal fees and stamp duty to buy their own roof (and the walls to support it. Yes, even if they wish to remain de facto). Or maybe it's a room full of furniture you'd like to help them with—whatever, you may only get a few months' notice to start saving, so if you've caught them with condoms in their wallet, play it safe and start saving now.

Biggest advantages if you've had it tough: If you're coping with paying child support after a divorce, your kids are usually turning 16 about now, so payments are no longer compulsory. Kids are starting to support themselves—and in theory, they can help around the house—so your budgets can actually be better off than before they were born if they contribute.

Biggest advantages if you've been good or if you catch up: You've got no more time limits to worry about. This is the lap of luxury stage, easing off the work wagon and being more generous with friends and family than ever before. You should have a nice house, nice cars and no stress (except when the kids are at each other's throats of course, which never changes no matter how much cash you have).

Note: If you've stuck to your goals from the time you left school, you'll be able to reach this stage without too much hassle by your late twenties/early thirties—just like me—even earning 'under average' incomes.

Biggest traps: Failing to pay out your house before retirement, failing to plan for retirement, buying a car that will wear out in time for retirement (so a large chunk of your superannuation has to replace it later). This age group often considers buying a small business about now to ease them into retirement, so they're particularly vulnerable to getting ripped off with scam businesses or investments. (See chapter 13.) *But the biggest trap for this age group is in thinking it's too late to fix your problems.* Even if you can't catch up to 'wealthy' status, you can still guarantee yourself a comfortable lifestyle.

How to get it: Start from scratch—just like I did—and become debt-free and investment-secure in only five to ten years, by working through the next few chapters.

AGES 51 plus

Work should definitely be an option by now, done mainly because you enjoy the social interaction, the responsibility and the sense of purpose that go with it and not because you need money. Hours should be what you want on a casual, part-time or contract basis, not what you need, because you should have income from your investments by now—enough to support you.

Income from part-time work can be used instead of drawing from your investments for day-to-day expenses like groceries. Pension entitlements vary too often to be predicted, so anything you get from the government after age 55 should be considered to be a bonus.

Biggest advantages: Freedom from work and family obligations in order to travel or enjoy life from a higher level of maturity.

Biggest traps: Spending your lump sum superannuation payment so you can get the full pension. That's like saying, *I can't handle my money, so I'll blow it and make do with being poor.*

Yes, you do have your pension reduced for every dollar you earn from investment, but only by a portion. The rest stays in your pocket on top of your investment income. Do your sums when the time comes and prove it for yourself—free financial planners from your superannuation fund, bank or even Centrelink will help you work out a comfortable balance.

(If you suffer from ill-health: Support payments from Centrelink are called the Disability Pension. Eligibility is not limited to any particular age, so long as you have left school and are unable to work full-time because of ill-health. So if you suffer from chronic asthma, arthritis or other debilitating health problems, contact your doctor and Centrelink to apply. See Appendix VI: Pennies from Heaven for more information.) See also page 27, Biggest Traps for 41 to 50 year-olds.

HOW I CHEATED TIME

As unbelievable as the following statistics may seem, they are true and achievable. They should be fantastic news for people like you, who are already more energetic than me, simply by virtue of having made it this far into a budgeting book. (Budget books rarely held my interest.) Chances are, you're also earning at least 10% more than I was at each of these stages. So you should have no trouble matching—or even beating—me on many of these. Please have a go and let me know.

Financial achievement (fully paid off)	Suggested goal	How long it really took
AGES 15 TO 19:		
$1000 work wardrobe	Week after last exam	The next day
A steady job	12 months, but prepared to do part-time work in the meantime	P/T job in 2 weeks plus choice of 2 full-time jobs within 2 months
A reliable car	3 years on a single income	4 months
$5000–$10,000 deposit for property	12 months, assuming you're renting	3 months, living at home
AGES 21 TO 30		
First home purchased and paid out	5 to 8 years	3 years
AGES 31 TO 40 EITHER:		
Investment property(s) paid off **OR** other shares or investments up to $100,000 **OR** upgrade home, cars & furniture using mostly cash AND have about $40,000 in other investments	3 to 5 years	Investment property: 12 months saving followed by loan for 18 months as single income family Shares: $60,000 accumulated in under 18 months
AGES 41 to 65		
Extra investments $30,000 to $60,000 a year	No time limit now, you're master (or mistress?) of your corner of the world	I haven't got to this stage yet!

The work wardrobe: I cheated time by shopping at St. Vincent's op shops over a long period before I left high school—spending about $70 instead of about $1000. Take a smile and a bag full of your family's 'outgrowns' and you can often leave with a discount on your purchases or a couple of freebies in exchange.

I also avoided wearing my best clothes as often as possible before leaving school to make them last 'as new' until after my job interviews. And I asked for Coles Myer or Woolworths vouchers in lieu of pressies from rellies for my last birthday and Easter during Year 12 and using them to buy undies and shoes, not to mention all those sexy little extras that guys don't have to worry about, like stockings and makeup and frilly girly things.

The steady job: I cheated time by being prepared to do absolutely anything—anything legal, that is—until I found exactly the right job for me. In my case, that was working at a servo and later packing shelves at Woolies. Working at chain stores has an added advantage for the cash desperate. It's called *staff discounts*. That's one good point to consider when you're shortlisting your first employers.

My first car: I cheated time by buying a one-owner 1969 Ford Cortina from an old couple for $500 when I was 16. I got it dirt cheap for two reasons. They weren't allowed to drive it anymore because of their health, and it had been sitting so long under a tree in the backyard without maintenance that the engine had seized up for good. The replacement engine cost $600. New tyres, cheapie seat covers and ten fingernails and three bottles of cut and polish later, the total cost came to about $1400. I didn't mind the car being so old. It had no rust, it was structurally stronger than most modern small cars at the time, and it had heaps more experience on the road than I did.

Did you know?

I'd had my first car about two years when I pulled into my dad's driveway for a chat. The windscreen was a bit muddy and the button on my wipers didn't make the water spray up on the windscreen anymore, so Dad offered to hose the windscreen off for me.

'How much oil is she using?' he asked while I was waiting.

'None,' I laughed. 'It runs on petrol.'

'What about engine oil?'

'Engine oil? What's engine oil?'

I've never seen a bonnet go up so fast. Actually, first I discovered what that little lever under the steering wheel was for, and then I never saw a bonnet go up so fast.

Dad pulled out this disgustingly filthy metal stick from somewhere and seemed surprised that it was wet right to the full mark.

At the time, I couldn't understand what all the fuss was about. Then I got it. And I sorted the mystery of why my windscreen washer had stopped working.

The bottle was empty.

Basic furniture: I was 14 when I bought my first washing machine. Mum's had died, she was strapped for cash, and I had savings so it seemed logical. Be careful of warranties when buying electrical goods so far in advance if you're going to store them away but bear in mind that most non-electronic white-goods have long lifespans. That one lasted me 14 years.

By the time I was 18, I owned my own bedroom suite; a coffee table; a blanket chest; two big wall units packed with all the basics for the kitchen, bathroom and laundry; as well as the washing machine and a garden shed with an old wheelbarrow. Although I was rarely home—because I went camping often with my horses on my vacant land—I didn't fully move out for another two years, and by the time I did, I'm not sure if

Mum was ecstatic or devastated to see me go. She had stacks more room, but boy, did she miss all the stuff that she'd been using.

3

The Twelve Laws of Gold: Happiness in Financial Success

King Cyrus—who ruled Babylon after its invasion in the fifth century BC and who subsequently squandered much of the city's wealth until its ruin—was one of the first to learn on a grand scale that Gold does not live under the same roof as Happiness for very long without Discipline as the landlord.

Many modern lotto winners learn the same hard lesson. One day they're paupers, the next day they're millionaires, and a few years—or even months—later they're paupers again, often worse off than before they started, because they've put family or friends offside in the process.

It doesn't have to be this way. Whether you're asset-rich and happiness-poor, or asset-poor and happiness-rich, there's a very simple way to have both—just invite Discipline to move in with you and follow a dozen little rules which are practically common sense. Some of these you'll notice are adaptations for modern use of the 'Seven Cures for a Lean Purse' by George Clason (author of *The Richest Man in Babylon*), and some are the product of personal experience—lessons I had to learn the hard way.

I call them the Twelve Laws of Gold. And no, you can't break any of them, because they're the essence to surviving happily while you turn small coins into wealth.

It's not enough for you to be happy with your money. If your money's not happy with you, it won't hang around you for long.

1. Pay yourself first. Every pay you should put aside money for bills, Christmas, holidays, groceries and other living expenses so that you never have to worry about being caught short; but in your rush to make ends meet, don't neglect the most important debt: the one you owe to yourself. If you leave this to last, you're likely to skip it altogether. But you deserve a strong financial future, so make sure you get it—just save for it, either a little each pay, or as a 'virtual bill' which you pay into a term deposit or any other savings at least twice a year.

It doesn't have to be much—start at 3% of your cash in hand (net pay) for the period, work up to 5% as soon as you can, and then 10% by the end of your first year. Don't cheat by including your compulsory superannuation deductions as part of it. You can, however, include any extra home loan repayments you make. Or by increasing your superannuation deductions. Or investing in shares, bonds or debentures.

Extra car repayments can count too, because of the amount of interest you'll be saving, which is more than most small investments can achieve. (Don't be confused. You may need your car, but it's not exactly an investment. Investments appreciate in value, but a car depreciates.) Life insurance payments don't count, however, unless your policy guarantees a small payout on a pre-agreed date, in which case you can only count that percentage of your regular payment, which you'll get back when you turn a certain age.

People who fail to follow this rule are the ones who feel like they never seem to get ahead, no matter how hard they work; while people who abide by it are the ones who build wealth upon wealth, year upon year, no matter how humble their beginnings were.

2. Always be saving towards something. A piece of gym equipment, new bed sheets, a piece of furniture, an electric toothbrush—anything—just so long as it's something you need, something you'll use often, and something that will make you feel better after you achieve buying it.

People who fail to follow this rule are often the ones who don't appreciate their own achievements. People who abide by it, achieve a greater sense of accomplishment and usually go on to higher successes.

3. Splurge regularly—*a little and often* on yourself. I recommend a sanity allowance for little regular splurges to keep yourself sane and help ward off the budgeting blues. Aim for 5 to 10% of your net wage (see chapter 5 for details). And yes, you can cheat a little here by including your goals for rule 2, but you really should blow about 5% every pay on additional personal treats like magazines, takeaway lunches, naughty habits you can't give up or other extras. If you've got kids they'll need between 0.5% and 5% to share too.

Yes, it is better if everyone spends their sanity allowance wisely on things that will retain value or add comfort for the family, but wise spending of the sanity allowance should only be encouraged, not enforced (because everyone's sanity is purchased in different ways).

People who fail to follow this rule are usually the ones who can't stick to budgets very long, and are often grumpy and miserable in the process. People who abide by this rule may still suffer the budgeter's blues now and then, but it rarely lasts long and they seem to enjoy stronger and longer relationships with their more sympathetic and understanding partners.

4. Don't let your eyes be bigger than your wallet. You can't buy a new Porsche if you're on a pension, and you can't live in a mansion if you can't afford to keep the spa full. Everything you buy must be in proportion to your income. That doesn't mean you have to compromise on quality if you're on a low income—quite the opposite. Always look at quality first, and then compare prices. That goes for everything from a new house to a new toothbrush. For example, if one pair of runners costs $150 and lasts you three years and another pair costs $15 but lasts only six months, you'd be heaps better off with six cheap pairs as long as they're all as comfortable as the alternative.

This law also warns you not to be suckered into buying anything now, if you have to figure out how to pay for it later. Furniture or electrical appliance ads of the buy-now-and-don't-pay-anything-for-six-months kind can be the most dangerous for the budget-cautious. Read fine print carefully and ask about interest rates, minimum repayments and penalties for late payment.

Then work out your budget as if you're paying for it now anyway, because if you can't do it now—unless you're counting financial eggs which haven't been hatched yet—you're unlikely to be able to do it later either. (In which case, even a credit card can be more flexible and less expensive!)

Find other ways to cope until you can afford the piece of furniture—or whatever—that you're drooling over. If your current lounge is looking daggy, look out for a bargain couch cover or throw a sheet or blanket over it and dress it up with matching ribbons and bows. If the dining chairs are falling apart, screw them together again, borrow some from a friend or relative, or take your dinner into the lounge room and eat in front of the TV. Yes, you will have to put a little thought into each solution at times, but you'll be surprised at how inventive you can be.

Remember, these short-term fixes are meant to put a band-aid on your big problems until you build enough savings to either buy the *thingy* outright, or put a deposit on it and pay the rest off it later.

If your budget is already strictly balanced, then every dollar you have to pay in interest on your purchases means an extra $1.50 (approx.) that you have to earn to pay for it because of payroll tax and GST. Even if your budget is a bit loose and allows for a few extra coins to splurge on yourself every pay, you'll have to deprive yourself of little extras just to pay interest.

Most people I meet spend a minimum of $400 a year on credit card interest alone. That's roughly the equivalent of a long weekend away, three months worth of petrol, 60 takeaway meals or ten trips to the cinema for a family of four. So next time you consider putting something on credit, also consider what you'll be missing out on if you don't pay it off by the due date.

Guys—more often than gals—often confide in me that their motto is: if you can't afford it, put it on credit. We often have a good giggle over that until I show them what they're missing out on. One guy in his early thirties—we'll call him Ted—had a nice income, a nice house, nice car, nice lifestyle etc., but he complained that he worked long hours and didn't seem to be getting anywhere in overall wealth accumulation. Ted admitted he knew what the problem was—he was spending and not saving—but he wanted to save without compromising on how much he spent on his lifestyle. So I suggested a few changes to HOW he was paying for things—using much the same advice as in Case Studies 4 and 5 as well as changing the brands—not how much or what he chose to buy. On his $1800 a fortnight income, I found $370 a fortnight that was going to waste for no other reason than that he was financially disorganised. He'd been doing this for about five years and wasted $48,000: on his $20 hourly rate, this means he worked 2400 hours—nearly a whole year—more than he had to. When I showed him this—and after I picked him up off the floor—he got really excited and made a mid-year resolution to trim his flamboyant expenses as well. Ted not only increased his repayments to pay out his first home sooner, but also bought an investment home to pay out quickly and will be starting his shares portfolio soon with his first tax refund.

Bankruptcy is the worst case scenario for people who fail to observe this rule. On the other hand, people who abide by it become extremely disciplined. They have to be, because this is the hardest rule to follow. The more income you earn, the more tempting it seems to be to over-spend it.

Beware: Your entire standard of living is linked to your income. If you overextend yourself—as many formerly top business people have learned—you can blow not only your budget, but your mortgage, your car loans, your children's continued or private education, your investments for retirement and your day-to-day lifestyle. In short, everything that is dependent on your income can fall like little dominoes into the great money pit that waits for everyone who loses sight of their financial goals.

5. Don't be a Scrooge. Don't drive your family insane by hounding them constantly over minuscule budget savings. Typical examples of this include hounding them to switch off fluorescent lights and switch off TVs, videos or other appliances at the wall instead of just at the unit. This is false economy! Money management *shouldn't* be a major fuss. It should be just one more thing you have to do—like cleaning your teeth. By all means switch off lights when you're finished using them, but don't make your family hate you for it in the process. The whole idea of a budget is to handle your money so you can enjoy life. There's no point in saving money if it's Hell's own hassle doing it.

Money management shouldn't be a major fuss. The whole idea of a good budget is to enjoy life.

6. Do understand that one person in every couple is usually better handling money than the other. If you're the better budgeter, be patient and supportive of your partner. Lead by example, and be generous with your partner's sanity allowance. Offer to help them work out what they want before they want it and help them work towards getting it if they ask you to—just like the partners in life that you're supposed to be. But don't climb down each other's throats over how you spend your own allowances and never demand to know how your partner's sanity allowance is spent if you can't tell.

Everyone needs *some* money to spend on themselves; let them use their share however they need to until they come to understand what you're getting at—if indeed they ever do. Don't let lack of money skills fester up to grounds for divorce—remember, you didn't choose your partner for their money skills to start with, did you?

7. Do understand that you *will* have budgeting blow-outs. It's not a sin. If you've been trying to be careful, then a blow-out is probably a sign that you've been overly strict with yourself—or just plain unlucky with an unexpected expense. If you've blown out because you've been too strict with yourself, then just treat the incident like a holiday from your budget and rework the budget with a little more attention to your sanity allowance. Otherwise, put your budget blow-out down to poor planning or bad luck. Ever notice how if one car blows up, the other one seems to go out in sympathy? As one very wise baby-bib once said: 'Spit happens'. Just rework your budget, cutting back on savings and allowances until unexpected financial burdens are paid off.

8. Do look after your belongings to make them last. You'll save megabucks. For example: one solid, quality timber dining suite can last you 20 years or more. If it costs $1500, for the sake of an example, and if you look after it, then you could think of it as having an average cost of $75 a year with a resale value at the end that will probably be almost what you paid for it. But if you flog it around and use it as a dance floor every second party, it's more likely to last you five years at best and cost you an average of $300 a year with no resale value to make up for anything. The extra 15 years worth of use between these two situations at that rate would save you about $9500 on a 25-year $100,000 mortgage at 8% interest rates. *That's a whole year's worth of repayments in exchange for taking care of only one set of furniture!*

9. Do invest every idle dollar so your money breeds more money. This does include putting money into savings accounts, although there are much better ways to make your money breed faster, including term deposits, shares, bonds and debentures, which are all explained in later chapters. And yes, you can cheat by 'parking' idle dollars into your home loan offset account—if you have one—so your home loan interest is reduced. You can also include any extra repayments you make which actually go off the loan balance, because as I've already explained, every dollar you save in interest is about $1.50 you don't have to earn.

10. Insure against losses. This law refers to your ability to step back from a situation and try to judge if there will be repercussions that might bite you in the backside later—like planting a palm tree under the eaves of your house or a leaky pond uphill from your foundations. It also includes thinking about contents, building and car insurance—depending on the value of the goods involved.

There's very little point, for instance, in paying $350 comprehensive insurance every year for a car that's worth less than $1000 on a good day. You could choose not to insure it at all—since CTP (compulsory third party) is already paid through your rego to cover you against any injuries you might cause to other people or property. Or you might prefer paying only for third party, fire and theft.

And, if you own a car, then carrying a mobile phone with you could save you A LOT if you leave your car broken down by the roadside and come back to find it stolen or vandalised. In this case, the mobile phone is also insurance. Naturally, the extent of the 'insurance' depends very much on the quality and value of the asset that you need to protect.

If you don't pay insurance, you should bank the same amount it would cost you into a savings account to pay for repairs to your current car if it's lost or stolen. If that never happens you'll have a great deposit for your next car.

To decide which way to go and what kind or how much insurance you need for anything, just imagine that your asset— whatever it is—has just been sucked into another dimension and you have to replace it. Then ask yourself, how are you going to afford replacing it, and what could you have done to ensure that you can get it back safely next time. (Like engraving a distinctive mark somewhere it won't be noticed.) For car security options, see chapter 10.

11. Ensure a future income. Here's the rule with the widest choices of solutions. Choose them all if you like—or even just a handful—by diversifying into stockmarket shares, investment homes, franchising your business, or paying into superannuation—most of which are much easier than they sound. (*Note:* This does *not* include taking part in pyramid selling schemes, which are unreliable, not to mention illegal.)

Also choose to stay up to date with legislation, including changes which may affect your assets. Sell off or expand your assets to maximise the growth potential of your investments as you judge fit.

Yes, you can hire a financial advisor to hand over the worry with the responsibility of handling investment decisions, but people who don't make any decisions themselves will be missing out on the greatest pleasure a budgeter can have: the pleasure of control over your financial destiny.

12. Never sell a reliable, comfortable car (under eight to ten years old) unless it's profitable to do so. Many low to middle-income people habitually upgrade their new car every few years—even if they're not business people and don't have tax incentives for doing so—because they've heard that maintenance costs and depreciation of their current car will undermine their ability to ever be able to afford a new replacement car again.

For example, one fellow I knew spent up to $15,000 (plus interest) upgrading his car to the latest model every two and a half years so his car was always under warranty and so he could sell it with a small amount of warranty 'on the clock'. He looked at it as if he was getting a $40,000 to $50,000 brand new car for only $15,000 every two and a half years. But this also suggests that he'd suddenly be expecting more than $6000 every year in maintenance costs on a car that's been well-maintained. (They have to be well-maintained to keep their warranties valid.) And I'd suggest that if a car fell apart that quickly, it should never have been worth $40,000 to start with.

Yes, there's depreciation to consider too, but the interest he pays on his car loan makes up for it.

My point is, he can choose to be someone who invests $6000 a year for eight years, leaving him with a car that's still worth about $6000 at the end, with at least $54,500 in the bank ready to buy a new one. (The $40,000 car is likely to cost about $52,600 by that time after inflation, so he should be able to do it with money left over.)

OR he can be someone who spends $47,800 in that time, and although he'll have a car that's possibly got a private sale value of about $40,000, he still has nothing in the bank to help him buy the new one and has a commitment to another $15,000 loan that he needs to keep him going.

Obviously, once you're financially successful there is not enough between these options to persuade you either way; it will be a matter of personal choice. But until then you could pay the money off a mortgage as additional payments instead of upgrading your car regularly. Doing this could—almost by itself—buy your freedom from debt long before your current car is eight years old. (And that's without any of the tips from my first book!)

4

Lazy Budgeting that Does Everything Except the Dishes

That dirty word: Blechh! *Budget* really is a dirty word, isn't it? It practically belongs in the same bin as *tax return, diet* and *dentist*, wouldn't you agree?

Or does it?

Imagine yourself for a moment as the multimillionaire you'd like to be: sitting back, sipping tequila under a poolside palm tree adjacent to your penthouse, listening to your favourite band give a personal performance while you eenie-meenie-minie-moe which one of your competitors you're going to buy out this week.

Now let's see . . . One million dollars a year coming in (after tax). You're still a tad careful with your cash, so let's say only ten grand in expenses and bills; $30,000 for a few wild parties instead of a world holiday this year; nine hundred grand for a comfortable shack and a set of wheels for the garage (yes, new ones every year for the collection); leaves you with . . . hmmm . . . a thousand bucks a week for play-money. Think you can handle that?

You do realise, however, what you just did? Yes, I tricked you. You just worked out your first budget . . . And it really can be just as simple as that. More to the point, it doesn't matter how much money you earn, or how much money you spend, you already have a budget whether you work it out and stick to it or not. That includes everyone—from children just learning what a dollar coin looks like to major multinational corporations with multi-billion dollar turnovers. And there are successes and failures at every level in between. The failures fail for many reasons, but the successes all have one thing in common: they work out a budget and stick to it. So quit wasting time and do it now. I'll walk you through it completely in this chapter.

Special note

If you've already read my other book, *Your Mortgage and How to Pay it off in Five Years by someone who did it in three*, then you may be tempted to skip this chapter because you think you've already done it.

That's true to a point.

You've done all the hard bits—the basic calculations—but in response to the piles of enthusiastic readers' letters I've received, this chapter has a stack more tips, goes into it from a different angle, and is also a little more thorough.

The good things about a budget are:

* You only have to work it out once; after that it's just an occasional tweaking if something changes.
* It usually takes only about half an hour to work out.
* You don't have to give up anything that's really important to you.
* You can turn big financial dreams into reality.
* You always get what you want eventually.
* And you don't have to worry about money very much in the meantime.

All you do is work out your budget, then spend the same money on the same things, pay in pay out, until each of your goals is achieved.

Budgets are to your wallet what fat cells are to your hips.

You can deny you have them as much as you like, but if you don't work a little bit every day towards keeping them under control, then you'll have to work a lot harder at beating the 'blow-out' later on.

It can be as simple in practice as it is in theory. The only thing that makes it difficult is a lack of discipline, so we have to find ways to make that easier for you too.

Yes, doubters, you do have to be regularly vigilant with your budget *if* you're trying to squeeze the last cent out of your paypacket. But being vigilant doesn't have to be a major hassle, as you'll soon learn.

Unconvinced?
Thinking of piking on this chapter?

Then think about how many times you've looked into your wallet the day before your payday and wondered, 'Where the heck did it all go?' You had plenty a few days ago, but taxes, loans and a menagerie of bills just kept clawing it out of your wallet.

Then think about this: even if you earn a meagre $20,000 a year, if you work for five years, that's still $100,000 that will slip through your fingers.

Say it slowly: *one hundred thousand dollars.*

Makes you want to find the nearest cliff, doesn't it? Please don't. No matter how much has slipped through your fingers so far, this chapter will help you put an end to it.

This'll only take about half an hour. So, stick the kettle on. Get a pencil and paper. And get your backside back here, pronto. Go ahead, I'll wait. (I take my coffee black with a pinch of salt, by the way.)

Okay then. Are you ready?

WHERE TO START?
EVALUATING THE STARTING LINE: INCOME VS. EXPENDITURE

The first thing you have to do is evaluate your starting line— now, today—whether you're fresh out of high school, ten years into the workforce, or four years into retirement. Whether you're a budget beginner or a budget blower, you can draw a line under all your debts, investments and income, circle the totals, and start from scratch—right now.

INCOME

It doesn't really matter how much you earn, or where your money comes from—whether it's social security, an employer, investments, a trust fund or even pocketmoney from your parents—the first thing you have to do is add up how much money you earn each pay period. For the sake of simplicity, I'm going to use the Aussie standard of 'fortnightly (f/n)' pays, but you can use weeks, fortnights or months, depending on how often you get paid.

Also, to make this a lot easier for you, I've provided blank appendix pages at the back of this book for you to fill in with your own details wherever you need to do your own calculations. But if you prefer, you can shout yourself a snazzy little notebook in which to copy questions and work things out, so that you or your friends can re-use this book later on without having it look like it's been pre-digested. Cover and decorate your little notebook if you like with dollar signs (my favourite), motivational slogans or photos of your dream house or car.

Sure, it might sound pedantic to get you to work out your own calculations so thoroughly at each stage, but a little extra effort now will save you a lot later on.

Remember, we're aiming for lazy budgeting.
Do it once.
Do it right.
And you shouldn't have to do it again for years.

(Only minor tweaks are needed if your circumstances change; for example, a change in income or bills.)

You also get three major advantages by taking this little extra effort now:

- When you're finished, you'll have a complete and easy-to-update record to keep.
- If you haven't already done it, it'll make working through the previous book in this series (*Your Mortgage and How to Pay it off in Five Years by someone who did it in three*) not only faster, but monkey-easy.
- And best of all, when you're filthy rich—or even just financially free—you can look back on just how humble your beginnings were . . . and smile.

So, in Appendix I, or on the first page of your personal notebook—or even on a spreadsheet, if you prefer to work onscreen—under the heading INCOME list and total your net fortnightly income. Include in this figure only your regular and reliable income. This may come from employers, social security (also known as the dole or Centrelink payments), investments, trust accounts, your parents or guardians, or even from superannuation funds.

Don't worry about the gross amounts here; we're only worried about the money that you actually have control over spending each fortnight. So if your pay also has compulsory union fees, compulsory employer-subsidised health insurance or any other 'practically permanent' deductions, then so much the better—you won't have to budget for them later in the section called predictable expenses. Please note however, that you shouldn't be including bank interest or hobby income at this stage, unless they provide regular amounts that you are already relying on every pay to survive. **Now underline the total per pay at the bottom of the page.**

Definition Alert!

Gross pay means *your total pay*, before tax and other compulsory deductions like superannuation, union fees etc. are taken out.

Net pay, strictly speaking, means the amount you actually get paid 'in the hand' or into your bank account after all your deductions (Christmas clubs, ambulance membership and health insurance etc.) have been taken out. But for the purposes of budgeting, we change the definition to mean *gross pay minus compulsory deductions only*. This makes it much simpler in the next section to adjust your budget when you shop around and find better deals on the others.

Employer subsidised: Some employers run compulsory superannuation or health funds for their employees where the employer 'subsidises' their staff's contributions by paying sometimes up to ten dollars into the fund for every dollar that is deducted from the employee's pay.

Example 1: Sally is a single mum, with a five-year-old daughter, Claire, and a 14-year-old son, Mike. Sally works part-time as a cleaner and types résumés at home as a paying hobby. She rents a small house with three bedrooms and a sleepout in Sydney's outer suburbs for a total of $540 a fortnight, but shares the rent with Jarod and Nicole, both unemployed, who contribute $160 a fortnight each. (This leaves Sally with only $220 a fortnight to pay, but still keeps her eligible for government rent assistance, in addition to her sole parent payments.)

Sally's income page in her notebook would look something like this:

Income per F/N:

Part-time income after tax and superannuation: $115.00
Child support from the children's fathers: $202.00
Sole parent and family payments etc. from
  social security: $479.20
Rental assistance: $ 90.20
Rent from sub-letting to tenants: $320.00
Total household income per f/n = $1206.40

Note that Sally's income from her typing hobby is not included here, as it is not regular or reliable enough for safe budgeting purposes. Such income is much safer added to her reserve bill paying account, or her sanity allowance.

Example 2: Harley and Tabitha are living in a de facto relationship, and have Harley's six-year-old son Ryan living with them. Harley is a casual boilermaker who earns $22,000 a year, while Tabitha is a part-time nurse earning $28,000 a year. They bought a tidy three-bedroom timber home in East Brisbane and now have a mortgage of $130,000 and a car loan of $12,000.

Their combined income page would look something like this:

Income for F/N:

Harley's wage (after tax and super have been
  deducted): $643.15
Tabitha's wage (after tax and super have been
  deducted): $792.30
Government family payments: $ 20.40
Total household income per f/n = $1455.85

Note: In this particular case, the child's non-custodial parent is not paying child support to the custodial parent, but if the mother had been paying child support, it would be included here, as it was in Example 1.

Obviously, these two families are finding it tough to make ends meet. But let me show you in this chapter how they can:

a)   meet all living expenses and . . .

b)   find savings of $3000 and $4000 a year respectively.

And that's BEFORE we even begin to look for ways to trim their budgets.

Special note for income sharers: If you're living in a marriage situation, where you share all income and expenses with your spouse or long-term de facto then you can save yourself even more trouble at this stage by making this a 'combined income' page—just as Harley and Tabitha have done in the second example.

But please let me repeat the warning to spare yourself the inevitable misery of combining incomes in order to cope with expenses where your best mate or close relatives are concerned, because unfortunately such arrangements seem only very rarely to succeed in the long term. Unless your relationship is a genuine union of hearts, souls and wallets, then it's a sad statistical fact that you're most likely doomed to failure when you share incomes, living expenses and major assets like cars, houses, vacant land and investment homes. And when friendships bust up, money complications only ever make things worse.

Naturally, there are a number of variations to the options you have available to keeping your finances 'clean cut' when living with friends or relatives—and I've explained a few of the most successful ways later in chapter 9: A Roof over your Head. All of them are adaptable, depending on individual incomes, personal tastes, mortgage situations and inter-family co-operation, but you should see enough hints to get your own creative juices flowing.

What counts is that each person feels in control of their own money, while still appreciating the value of the other person's contributions. And that goes for any couple—married or otherwise—or any bunch of mates who wish to pool their resources in order to afford a roof over their heads.

Now for stage 2 of evaluating your starting line: examining your expenditure.

EXPENDITURE

Assuming for the moment that you have no control over your permanent payroll deductions like tax, union fees etc., then the rest of your income should be prioritised for a) spending on urgent bills or current overdue debts, b) saving up for regular and future expected bills, c) saving a nest-egg for your future, and d) spending on yourself, your family and your home.

You can argue over the order in which to put them as much as you like, but you buy yourself no dignity—but plenty of headaches—if you have overdue bills or outstanding debts against you. So regardless of the order in which you deal with the other three points, current urgent debts need to be the first ones to attack.

CURRENT URGENT DEBTS

These are as simple as they sound. If you've been a good little black duck, then you'll be able to write nil in Appendix II— or on page 2 of your notebook—and skip right to the next section altogether. You can even give yourself a pat on the back, because 94% or more of the industrialised population on this planet live every day with at least some debt hanging over their heads—yes, even billionaires. (Actually, especially billionaires, who often borrow money to maximise tax benefits, including negative-gearing, while they multiply their assets!)

So unless you're either *really* fresh out of high school, a recent lotto winner, or just plain careful like Harley and

---

Definition Alert!

Negative-gearing: To borrow money for investing in shares or property etc., and then—where bank interest is higher than investment income—to use the difference between these two amounts as a deduction for tax purposes.

Tabitha in our previous example, then you'll have to list everyone you currently owe money to and should have repaid, but haven't yet because you can't afford it. That includes friends, relatives, credit cards, laybys, banks, landlords, money-lenders, and other finance or rental companies.

DON'T WORRY ABOUT YOUR STANDARD REGU-LAR LOAN REPAYMENTS HERE—we'll take care of them in the next section on predictable expenditure. What we're worried about at the moment is discouraging the hired thugs from stalking you. After all, you'll want both your legs in work-ing order if you're going to enjoy being rich later, won't you?

Now, make sure when you fill out your list of current urgent debts that you include all the due dates and the minimum repay-ments allowed for each. For example, you might owe $856.38 on your credit card, but the minimum monthly repayment is only $25, so you'll need to note both amounts. For example:

Example 1: Sally & children
Current urgent debts

Item	Total owing	Minimum repayment	Due date comments	Urgency ranking
Credit card	$856.38	$25.00	18th of each month	☹☹
Layby (Claire's school books)	$ 41.20	$5.00/week	Claire goes back to school in 2 weeks	☹☹☹
Landlord owed part of last. week's rent	$ 40.00		Any time soon, so long as I don't miss any more	☹☹
I.O.U. friend for lotto	$ 20.00	—		☹
Big Clyde's FastCash owed for the playstation Sally bought Mike for his birthday	$250.00	$50.00 OR ELSE!	Every 2nd Friday	☹☹☹☹☹
Rent-a-Thingy owed part of last month's TV & refrigerator hire	$ 12.00	$12.00	By next week, or another $8 fee is charged	☹☹☹
Totals:	$1219.58	$92.00		

Note: There is no example 2 for this section because Harley and Tabitha are both determined not to borrow money from friends or relatives and always pay all their bills in full before the due dates.

URGENCY RANKINGS

Sure, it's probably obvious from the table that if Sally doesn't pay Big Clyde his fifty bucks this week, then she's probably going to find walking fairly uncomfortable next week—a good reminder, if you're tempted, that at no time and under no circumstances (no matter how desperate you are) should you consult an obvious thug for cash. But ranking each of your urgent debts with a simple set of one to five-star symbols can certainly help you sort out priorities where the less urgent debts are concerned. It's also particularly useful—as you'll discover before the end of this chapter—to have a good idea where your priorities need to be when you're trying to stretch your pitiful paypacket over considerable debts (as our poor Sally is in this example).

You can rank your urgent debts with any symbols you prefer—dollar signs, asterisks or little cartoons of debt collectors if you like, but for the sake of our example, I've used little frowny faces:

URGENCY RANKING LEGEND

☹   Fairly flexible repayments. You're mainly driven by guilt to repay. But the longer you leave it, the less likely you are to get a Christmas card from these guys next year.

☹☹   You've been naughty, repayments are overdue, but still flexible and without late fees.

☹☹☹   You have a non-negotiable deadline where repayments must be made or you'll be charged fines or miss out on goods or discount periods.

☹☹☹☹   Payment must be made in full by a set date, or you'll get slugged with heavy fines or penalties OR miss out on big discounts for early payment.

☹☹☹☹☹ Pay up, or learn a new definition of pain.

Now, the only thing that's stopping you from figuring out how to get rid of all this existing debt is the impending doom of bills that you haven't yet received. So before we finish off here, we have to get cracking with the last stage of lazy budgeting: predictable expenditure.

PREDICTABLE EXPENDITURE

Some days, life gets so complex and you feel so small in the scheme of things that the only way you might realise that you're still alive is that somebody keeps sending you bills. The bad news is that if it ever stops, then you probably are dead. The good news is that if you understand, predict and control your regular expenses, then you can not only learn to live happily with your expenses, you can actually plan to have extra cash left over for spoiling yourself—or for investing, like a clever little mini-mogul.

Definition Alert!
Mini-mogul

n. Author's terminology for a young mogul or tycoon in training; a rare and complex specimen, often heard declining an expensive night out on the town with friends, but also renowned for their spending power. A mini-mogul accumulates cash and assets at the rate of 60% to 80% of their net income, and has major financial institutions falling over themselves to lend them money (not to mention queues of fair-weather friends lining up to borrow money!).

So in Appendix III—or on page three of your notebook— list all of your predictable expenditure, no matter how often it occurs. For example, your power bills may be charged quarterly (every three months), but your phone bill might bomb your mailbox every month. The idea is that once you know how often your bills arrive—and roughly how much to expect each time—you can figure out how much you have to put aside every pay in order to cope with the bills when they arrive.

(Instead of having a panic attack and driving around town to find the tallest building to jump off.)

Don't sweat too much over bills—like power and phone, which vary to some extent from bill to bill depending on your usage—we'll factor in a safety net to cope with that later. All you should be worried about now is remembering to include every one of your regular expenses without missing any. Because there are few things in life as utterly deflating as an unexpected *Goliath* of a bill that bombs your mailbox about two seconds after you've just bought the sound system that you've been drooling over since birth. So to save you the embarrassment and to help jog your memory, I've included a list of suggestions in Appendix III.

Please note that this stage is about as difficult as budgeting gets. And it's not really so much difficult as it is *annoying* to dig through all your old accounts to find out how much you had to pay for each of them last time. But if your memory is as lousy as mine is, then I'm afraid that's exactly what you'll have to do, because we don't want to have to do this again for a long time, so we'll just have to get it right the first time. Okay?

Please also note that you don't have to include your consumables, like groceries, car fuel, meals at work or other 'out of wallet expenses' at this stage. You can if your budget is fairly uncomplicated—and if you're completely disciplined with your expenses—otherwise you can monitor these more carefully as part of your 'disposable income', which is explained next. If you're unsure, then just write them towards the bottom of your list where they can be easily totalled up together later.

Now hang on! Just before you bolt off to scour the house for old bill statements, let me run through our two examples first, to illustrate a few tricks and shortcuts.

Firstly, if you're just starting out (or planning to move out on your own), and if you've never received a power, rates or phone bill before, then ask your parents how much they usually pay at home. Make an educated guess from that, or ask the billing companies for their help in working it out. Don't get too carried away here. It won't matter if you're a little out the first time, just so long as you have something stashed aside to help your budget cope when the first bills start rolling in.

First, let's look at the case of Sally, who is renting and has two children but no car:

Bills	$ per year	$ per F/nly pay
ANNUAL LIVING EXPENSES:		
Contents insurance	180	
Phone (home & mobile total)	600	
School books & other public education costs	220	
Medical: contraception, gym fees, vitamins & medicines.	650	
Vet shots, worming, flea treatments etc. for Fido	240	
Sub-total:	1890	
Rounds up to a fortnightly cost so far of:		**$73**
+ OUT OF POCKET EXPENSES PER FORTNIGHT:		
House rent		540
TV, fridge and washing machine rental from Rent-a-Thingy		85
Meat & groceries		260
Buses, taxi fares & trains		45
Meals at work		18
Pocket money for children (Claire $1/wk; Mike $5/wk)		12
Clothes, haircuts or treats		30
Union fees part-time rates (automatically deducted from paypacket)		3
Christmas savings		20
Sub-total expenses per fortnight:		**$ 1086**
Add a safety net for inflation and round up:	+	**$ 4**
Total basic living expenses per fortnight:		**$ 1090**

Note: Sally's part-time income—as previously mentioned—is $1206.40 per fortnight, so she has a budgeting surplus of $116.40 every pay, totalling $3026.40 a year!

Yes, she is budgeting carefully and sharing rent to achieve this surplus—and for a while she'll have to use most of it to clear her debts—but she scores free babysitting by arrangement with her roomies in exchange for the freedom to work a few hours to keep her skills current. (Since travel and meal costs at work eat almost half of her net income, there's little other reason she would choose to work, aside from social interaction and self-esteem.)

The point of including this list in addition to illustrating the following tips is to get you thinking about finance and lifestyle options. For instance, it's fairly obvious that if Sally moves away from Sydney to where housing is considerably cheaper, she can have the same amount of money without having to work or share rent with anyone. (Of course, there may be good reasons why she doesn't feel she can move—the children's access to their fathers, for instance. But it's surprising how often people don't even stop to consider such options.) Using her first batch of savings to buy electrical goods instead of renting them becomes the next most obvious step and so on. (See Case Studies in chapter 17 for more examples.)

For now, let's get back to the tricks and shortcuts for working out YOUR budget:

Trick 1: You'll notice we saved a little time in calculations by thinking about predictable bills in two groups: 'Annual living expenses' which can be grouped as big bills throughout the year; and 'Out of pocket' expenses, which siphon your account dry as fast as you can top it up.

Trick 2: Listing expenses like this should shock you into realising just how much cash really slips through your wallet every pay. You've probably already spotted a few ways that Sally can plug her money leaks. For instance, we know that Sally has a household income of $1206.40 a fortnight. Her basic living expenses are only $1090.00 a fortnight, which means she should have $116.40 every pay to treat herself, treat her children and to save for the future. But does she?

No.

She's not only in debt to her credit card, friends and laybys, but she's had to hock her dignity to a loan shark as well. Obviously, she's blowing her budget not only regularly, but thoroughly—and we'll get to solutions for that problem very soon. The trick for now is, having fed your think-tank a few easy-to-absorb facts, we should have it subconsciously starting to solve a lot of Sally's—and your own—budgeting booboos.

On the subject of laybys

I meet so many people who are proud of the fact that they live quite nicely without a credit card, yet wonder why their budgets keep blowing out of control. The answer is very often laybys. For budget beginners, a layby is where a shop puts aside whatever thingy it is you want to buy on the basis that you don't get it until you've paid it off with weekly or fortnightly repayments. Aside from having to find money in budgets for these unexpected expenses, sometimes with less reputable stores—if you stop making repayments—it's possible you won't get your thingy OR your money back. In such cases, laybys are more dangerous than credit purchases. They are—in my vocabulary—just the flipside of the plastic because my definition for both is the same: *Buy now what you can't afford, and figure out how to pay for it later.* The only difference is, the credit card has more safety features. (See chapter 8: How to House-train your Credit Card.)

Trick 3: A small safety net is added to help cope with inflation and bigger than expected bills throughout the year AND to keep our total figures easy to work with. Four dollars may not seem like much, but it's the equivalent of $104 a year, so it makes for a good start while Sally tries to work herself out of the money pit that she's dug for herself.

Later, when she's on top of things and all her old debts are paid, she can afford to round it up a little more if she wants to. But generally speaking, a safety net of between $4 and $20 is all that most people would need every fortnight, because you save it until you need it.

Example 2: Harley is our casual boilermaker from East Brisbane who's into netsurfing, while his de facto Tabitha is a part-time nurse who likes handicrafts. Between them, they own one car and are paying off a second car in addition to their mortgage.

Their combined predictable expenditure table would look something like this:

Bills	Amount per year	Amount per F/N
ANNUAL LIVING EXPENSES:		
Rates = $420, four times a year	1680	
Phone (home & mobile total)	1200	
Electricity/gas	790	
Car registration $490 + $320	810	
Car insurance	680	
Car repairs/servicing on average over last five years*	1600	
House & contents insurance	400	
Education costs (for 2nd hand school books & uniforms for Ryan)	200	
Meat** (see also *Did you know?* p. 62)	420	
Medical: contraception, gym fees, vitamins & medicines	600	
Union fees total	270	
Clothes and haircuts**	700	
Vet bills	120	
Christmas savings	500	
Other: holiday savings	1000	
furniture savings (all their stuff is old, so they try to upgrade one room every year. This year, they're saving for a big new fridge.)	990	
Rounds to a fortnightly cost so far of:		460
+ OUT OF POCKET EXPENSES/FORTNIGHT:		
Health insurance		nil
Rent/mortgage repayment/housekeeping contribution		460
Credit card repayment including extra for interest. (*Note:* this is NOT your minimum repayment. It's how much you need to pay in order to pay off your credit card in a few months—not a few years!) This couple doesn't use credit cards.		nil
Car loan		155
Groceries, excluding meat**		220
Kid's pocket money (Ryan pays for his own sports club membership and occasional cinema tickets with this, as well as snacks at school.)		30
Other: Newspapers/magazines/lotto etc.		10
Takeaway dinners		40
Meals at work		nil
Harley's sanity allowance		25
Tabitha's sanity allowance		50
Plus safety margin		5.85
Total of all bills for the year:	$	**$1455.85 F/N**

Note: This family's income—as mentioned earlier—is $1455.85. So even before they begin to consider streamlining and re-organising their finances, they can still be assured that all expenses can be paid PLUS they'll have holiday, Christmas and furniture savings totalling $2500 a year PLUS a cosy safety margin of nearly $150 a year and holiday and sanity allowances (part of which can be saved) of up to $2950.

Total savings possible are $2650 a year without even trying hard!

* If you have no idea how much you've spent on car repairs, maintenance and servicing in the last five years, then try using the following generalised amounts—as suggested by my mechanic but excluding GST—until you have a better idea of expenses for your own car: 0–5 year-old car: $300 a year; 5–10 year-old car: $800 a year; 10 year or older car: $1500 a year.

** I've included clothes, haircuts and meat here because Tabitha likes to save up for them as regular expenses and buy them infrequently throughout the year so she can get better discounts. I do this too, and if you wish to join us in buying meat this way, then remember not to include it in your grocery calculations.

Notes: Because Harley's wage is casual and slightly less predictable, he manages their holiday savings account manually, borrowing from it if his pay is short one pay, and topping it up when he works extra hours. He does this without any effort by having his pay go into his personal savings account, setting up automatic transfers to pay his car loan and contribution to the home mortgage—he takes out the same small amount for his wallet every pay—and whatever's left in his account is automatically considered to be their holiday savings. People who are self-employed can do something like this too, if their incomes are similarly unpredictable.

Please note that there is no need to be completely accurate at this stage. You can round up each bill to the nearest dollar— or even five dollars if you like—just as long as you make every effort not to underestimate. It won't worry you too much, I'll bet, if your bill paying account is a little over-stuffed. But it certainly might worry you if there's not enough in there to cope when all your bills arrive at once (which they notoriously tend to do by the way, usually between Christmas and New Year!).

So off you go, flip to Appendix III and fill in all your regular expenses. (Be careful when checking old bills for how much you paid last time to make sure you include any price increases that you may already be warned about. And make sure you remember to multiply each bill total by the number of times you receive it each year. For example, if your last rates bill was for $350.00 but you pay rates four times a year, then make sure you put $1400.00—four times $350.00—into the rates column, instead of just $350.00.)

Beware, this list is not comprehensive. Everyone spends their money slightly differently, so it might be a good idea for you to take a break right about now—overnight even, if your brain cells are overheating—so you can recharge the old think-centre and figure out if I've missed any expenses that apply to you.

Did you know?

You can buy meat in bulk from independent butchers for a party discount or bulk discount—sometimes even from major chain stores, if you just ask.

Do also consider buying meat on the hoof about once a year—even if you live in the city—especially if you have bone-loving dogs. Aside from the great life experience for the family to take them to a cattle sale, it will halve your beef and petfood bill. You can buy a small to medium beast for about $200 to $300 and arrange transport for it direct from the saleyards to an independent butcher's slaughteryards at a cost of about $20 to $60 (and the driver handles all your permits for travelling stock). Butchering fees are between $0.80 and $2.00 a kilo, so a family that spends about $30 to $50 a fortnight in beef will be about $15 to $25 a fortnight better off and get about six months worth of pet mince and bones for Fido as a bonus. *Note:* Cattle prices are almost reliably lower in the last sales before Christmas and Easter public holidays.

Just make sure you give your butcher a few days' notice before you go to the sales. Also go to at least one auction before you buy, so you have an idea of how much a beast is worth before you stick you hand in the air. (Some sales work by the kilo, so you have to go to the weighing area and watch there too.) Ask your butcher or the auctioneer about farmers who can transport your beast from the sales to the butcher's yards for you. Make sure you have a big chest freezer empty, but don't start it cooling too early, as it will be about a week before you pick up your meat. Then prepare yourself to ignore all those big black eyes staring at you from the holding pens—and just pick and pay about once a year.

CRUNCH TIME, PUTTING THE FIGURES TOGETHER

Well, you've done most of the hard work by now. To summarise and to nut out your lazy budget from here, there are six simple steps:

1. **Total your income:** Write down how much you earn each pay 'in the hand'. Eg.: Your net pay after tax, super and union fees, if any, have been taken out = Answer A.
2. **Total your current urgent debts:** List all your existing overdue bills taking note of minimum payments due and deadlines. Then decide how much you can afford to repay each fortnight to get rid of them—making sure your repayment plan will be okay with the person who sent you the bill. The total of your fortnightly repayments on all urgent debts = Answer B.
3. **Total your 'out of wallet' consumables:** List and add

together your weekly consumables—ie. your groceries, fuel, public transport, meals at work, and other weekly cash purchases. This = Answer C.

4. **Save up for future bills:** Write down your total foreseeable bills for the year and divide it by the number of times you get paid. That gives you an average amount to stick into a bill paying account every pay at your local bank, building society or credit union. By the way, if your bills exceed your income at this stage, then you're in deep trouble! (Pay particular attention to the budgeting tips later on.) The amount you stick aside for bills every pay = Answer D.

5. **Calculate your disposable income:** Using your answers from above, take B, C and D away from A to get your answer E. This is your disposable income. This is what you can afford to spend on yourself, your family, your home and your nest-egg. And this is where the fun begins.

6. **Create a wish list:** Choose up to five things—depending on cost—that you would like to buy in the next three, six or 12 months by budgeting your disposable income carefully. Ring around for prices so you have a closer idea of what your target is—flip to the chapter about your sanity allowance if you want to clue up on more tricks and hints.

7. **Then go for it . . . don't blow it.** (Your disposable income, that is.)

Sooo many people fall flat on their financial faces because they simply lose track of what they want in life. Please, *please* don't be like that. This book is your opportunity to catch up and get ahead with the benefit of someone else's hindsight. Please use it and spread the word around.

Income – expenditure (weekly living expenses + predictable bills averaged over each pay + repayments of current urgent debts) = sanity allowance.

ARE YOUR EYES BIGGER THAN YOUR WALLET?

After doing the calculation in the previous section, you will know that your eyes are bigger than your wallet if you look at how much your disposable income is every pay and feel a burning desire to invent a new swear word.

Where the heck, you might wonder, *can all that money go every week?*

Newsflash: You spend it.

Believe it or not, it is actually possible to get a very good feeling in the pit of your tummy whenever you look at your disposable income if you're able to remember all the new and pleasurable things or experiences your money has been traded for, instead of wondering where it disappeared to.

That's where the sanity allowance comes in.

Before we get to it, however, you might be feeling a little cheated by this stage if your living expenses are so great and your income so small that your leftover disposable income is an insult to the standard of life you want to live. If this is the case, skip to chapter 15: Give Yourself a Money Make-over where you'll find stacks of hints and tips for solving this dilemma.

Budgeting works for anyone who earns money. It doesn't matter where the money comes from—your parents, the dole, or a job—be it part-time, casual or full-time.

Naturally, the more you earn, the greater your buying power. But what's more important is the less you earn, the more careful you have to be to make your budget work.

The aim of this book is to:

Make sure you spend most of your money on things that build wealth, and still have money left over for yourself.

**Despite the rising cost of living,
it's still surprisingly popular.**

5

Your Sanity Allowance

> **Strict budgets are like strict diets . . . You only need one if you've been naughty.**
>
> **Your sanity allowance is your once-a-fortnight chocolate bar.**
>
> **It's a regular treat for being good. It also makes sure you get all the little things you want when all the big things are sucking your wallet dry.**

If you want to stay sane—whether you're deliberately budgeting or not—then you must always spend a small amount every pay on treats for yourself and for your family.

It's why you work.

If you didn't want a comfortable lifestyle for yourself and your family, then you might as well sell up and go feral. But in trying to achieve financial success, you'd be surprised how many people seem to think that 'budgeting' means that you have to give up on all the little special treats that you enjoy.

It's the OPPOSITE, people!

The idea is to have FUN—to wake up in the morning with a whopping great grin on your face that an army couldn't remove with a ballistic missile.

And it's easy to do:

- **Just work out what it is in life that you really enjoy.**
- **And make sure you always have money available to do those things.**

That way, you won't feel any pain in cutting back on everything else. Who cares, for instance, what brand of soap powder you wash your clothes in if it does the job, is environmentally friendly and leaves coins in your wallet while you still enjoy your favourite imported coffee at morning tea?

But if you're like me, treats can get out of hand. You either skimp too harshly or go overboard, and both situations can be bad for you. That's why I use and recommend a regular sanity allowance.

Did you know?

If I had a dollar for every person who's told me that I must have lived on bread and water to pay off a mortgage in three years I'd buy a Ferrari and a spare garage to park it in!

It's the exact opposite.

The whole idea of budgeting is to make sure you get everything you want as soon as possible. Yes, if you've been naughty and let debts creep up, you may have to punish yourself for a few pays by cutting back, but never deny yourself the things you enjoy. Life's too short.

HOW MUCH?

No matter what size your income or how loose or strict your budget is, each person in the family should have a sanity allowance for personal treats; and although careful budgeting of this should be encouraged, it shouldn't be enforced. For the kids, you'll probably call it pocketmoney and you can attach to it whatever chores lists you like. But no matter who it's for, it rarely needs to be anything more than $25 a week. (Or about $40 a week if you're either single with an income over $60,000 or a couple earning $90,000 a year or more. *Note:* These figures are my personal guide. Do what's comfortable for you.)

Do try to keep it over $10, however—even if you're only earning pocketmoney from your parents—because you won't be able to avoid a budget blow-out for long if you feel strangled or enslaved by your budget. You'll spend money just for your sanity's sake.

This is not to say that you should 'waste' your sanity allowance regularly on trivial purchases—although you should be free to do this without having to answer to anyone, if that's what it takes to spoil yourself that particular fortnight. The intended purchases for this allowance are completely flexible. You can spend your sanity allowance regularly and in full each pay, or you can save all or some of it for bigger splurges, as I used to when I needed a new saddle, CD player or something for around the house.

MORE HELP CHOOSING
To help decide how to budget your sanity allowance, make two columns. One is for things that cost $40 or less, and the other is for $40 or more. I chose $40 as an example because that's about the cost of a fortnight's worth of fuel for an average car, and by comparison, that's roughly what most people seem to need to stay sane. When fuel goes up—again—you should try to keep your sanity allowance 'up' to a similar figure; after all, as fuel goes up, it's going to take a little more effort every pay to keep you sane, isn't it? (Don't think you can't afford it. I'm here to show you how you can.)

Suggestions for the $40 or less column—probably the hardest column to fill—include:

- The 'corny' card night with friends—which is as much fun as you make it.
- Any sport that doesn't induce a groin strain just thinking about it.
- Netsurfing at home, or at your local library—where you can also check out non-virtual specimens of the opposite sex.
- A movie at Imax or your favourite multiplex.
- Anything else that doesn't involve a wallet assassin.

Definition Alert!
Wallet assassins

Wallet assassins are the demons conjured up by others to suck megabucks out of our pockets either:
- **By getting us addicted to them, like chocolate, alcohol and cigarettes.**
- **Or by making us feel unworthy if we don't have them, like a new car every few years. If it bugs you to see someone else in a flashier car than your reliable jalopy, try thinking, 'Mmm yes, that's a nice debt you're driving.'**
- **By advertising products at great expense— usually by sticking a major sports star in the ad, and then passing the expense on to us. 'Big name' brands are usually the worst offenders, so compare value for price when buying anything over $10. (Just make sure to look for sloppy stitching, glueing, or joining of any pieces that look weak and make sure you're not sacrificing quality for the sake of the money saved.)**

Into your second column—the $40 and over list—go all the things that you really, *really* enjoy, but that cost more than a tank of fuel to indulge in: ie. nightclubbing with friends, buying computer games, daytrips to local tourist sites, skydiving, snowskiing etc. Then say goodbye to them, because you won't be doing them anymore. *Kidding!* Of course, you can do them. You're just going to budget for them, do them less often— maybe once a week, fortnight, month or season, depending on their expense—and use them as a reward for sticking to your goals. In fact, you can have just about anything you can think of, provided you are prepared to wait and budget for it or sacrifice something else.

FINANCIAL RULES TO SUCCESS

1: To avoid a braincell blow-out, always budget to have fun.

Clause 1 to Rule 1: Don't go out hoping fun will happen to you. Go out determined to have a great time with friends.

Subclause 1a of Clause 1 to Rule 1: Don't have fun by annoying other people because you can't have fun again tomorrow if you're behind bars.

Subclause 1b to Clause 1 of Rule 1: Don't have fun by doing anything that involves a fine if you're caught, because you can't afford it and your friends won't bail you out because they have all read this book too.

2: There's no shame in being poor, only in behaving poorly.

WHEN EXPENSIVE HOBBIES ARE YOUR TREATS

If you have seriously expensive hobbies—like competition motor sports for instance—then firstly, make sure you can afford it. Try to evaluate if you're being pressured into the sport by friends and whether you're attempting to live a Mercedes lifestyle without the Mercedes income to support it.

If you'd rather cark it than give up or cut back on your expensive hobbies in the short term, that's okay too. It will be your personal decision to give up other life goals so you can continue to afford them. You can't have everything on a low income. Just budget for the costly hobbies separately from your sanity allowance. Reduce your sanity allowance a little to compensate—perhaps by 20%—and treat your major hobby expenses more like monthly bills that must be saved up for. Also seek sponsorship from local businesses in exchange for advertising wherever possible to reduce your costs.

Then make sure you appreciate the fact that you're doing what you love, and don't take it for granted. Because—depending on your income—you will probably have to compromise for a much smaller sanity allowance if you have a family who is also dependent on your income.

WHEN YOU'RE ON A LOW OR VERY LOW INCOME

I've been here, so I know surviving can be tough. You do have to be more careful with your sanity allowance—not so much with *how much* you allow yourself, but more importantly, *what* you use it for.

As Case Study 1 in chapter 17 shows later, you can boost your self-esteem significantly by replacing trivial impulse purchases with deliberate shopping choices. That's the first step to surviving on a low income: ensuring your money gets you what you want to keep you happy.

The next step is to shift the focus of your budget.

Where you might have budgeted separately in the past so you could afford lotto, magazines, newspapers, trips to the cinema and takeaway meals etc. as a regular part of your lifestyle, you might now have to consider them as treats and pay for them out of your sanity allowance. Doing this will very quickly make you appreciate the value of these items in your life, and appreciating them is the biggest step towards enjoying the feeling of spending your money.

This is the heart of this book.

> In my experience, you appreciate the joy of spending money the most not when you're wealthy but when you don't have much and have to plan ahead and work hard to get what you want.

In that respect, even high-income earners could do well to budget strictly for a short period—or perhaps two pays every year, or maybe two to three consecutive months every five years or so—as a matter of discipline to stay aware of excesses. Savings from these self-inflicted budget restrictions then create a surplus which can be splurged either as an extra personal or family treat, invested for the future, or given as gifts to friends or charity.

> **Yes, I still recommend sticking to a firm budget once you're financially comfortable—just as any successful multinational company would.**

FOR PEOPLE ON HIGH INCOMES OR *PLANNING TO BE* ON HIGH INCOMES OR WITH UNEXPECTED WEALTH

I've been here too, so I know that the larger your income, the faster your expenses can swell to consume it. It's easy to let large sums slip through your fingers without feeling it—*far too easy*. But this money will serve you better if you use it for regular new investments (hopefully with increasing portions as donations to charity or generosity to others).

Deliberate budgeting is the best and easiest way I've found to maximise the benefits of high incomes without the worry of having money gush from your pockets.

Yes, you do still need a personal sanity allowance. And yes, it should still be meagre—no more than $50 a week—as this is a matter of self-discipline, not scroogieness.

If you've come by your wealth unexpectedly, then this is especially important in the first 12 months of 'sudden wealth'.

'CAN'T BE BOTHERED' ARE THE FIRST THREE WORDS TO FAILURE

If you enjoy splurging your high income regularly, then that's okay too, but be warned. Budget what you think you need regularly into a splurge account. At the end of the year, you can either invest anything you haven't used, donate it and claim a tax deduction, or use it for being particularly generous to your friends and family at Christmas—and then start your splurge account from scratch again in the new year to ensure you stay disciplined AND get the best value for money.

Did you know?

My personal sanity allowance varies from $8 to $12 a week depending on the season, and is actually less than what it was when I was struggling ($20 to $25 a week).

This is not because I've gone all scroogie, but simply that my personal treats—you may have guessed many of these by now—don't cost more than this.

KEEPING TRACK

If you choose to spend your sanity allowance straight from your wallet, you shouldn't mix it with your other cash, because you could spend it by accident on other things. **Spending it on unexpected things is not a sin. Spending it accidentally is.** Regular treats are your 'condom' to protect you against blowing your budget. If your sanity allowance goes into your wallet, insulate it from your other cash by sticking it in a separate section or inside a plastic coin bag—the zippie-sealie kind that's hard to open 'accidentally'.

If you wish to spend your sanity allowance regularly and in full every pay: Withdraw it from your account by EFTPOS with your other money—to cut down on EFTPOS fees—and then store it in your wallet as I've just suggested, so you can always tell at a glance how much you have left.

If you wish to spend some and save some every pay: Save part or all of it for bigger treats that you can't afford with only one pay's worth of sanity allowance, by either keeping it in a coin bag at home, in a separate savings account, or 'park' it in your mortgage offset facility until you need it. (Don't make a big deal about parking it in the mortgage offset account by the way. You could park your entire $50 sanity allowance in it every month—spending it only on the last day of each month—and you'd still only save about $4 in interest over a whole year. So choose the option that's most *convenient* for you, because differences in investment returns will be insignificant.)

With all your spare income 'parked' in the offset account, it can be easy to lose track of your sanity allowance, so I actually prefer using a separate savings account. Never carry savings in your wallet or anywhere else where they could be easily lost or stolen.

MANAGING ONE ACCOUNT

As I've already mentioned, your sanity allowance—like all other portions of your budget—must be planned for. (Even if you plan for unplanned spending, as already discussed.) So although you can use some of it for little impulse splurges, it really is wisest if you plan ahead to spend it on little personal treats like makeup or tools for your workshop; buying birthday, wedding and anniversary presents; making small donations; buying lottery tickets; spoiling yourself occasionally with a dinner out. The choice is entirely yours.

All you have to do is:
* List your goal purchases in order of importance.
* Ring around for the going price.
* Divide the total costs by the number of pays you will get over the next two to six months to figure out how much you have to put away for each item in order to afford it.
* Sit back and wait for the money to accumulate.

Here's a handy little table you can use to help you record everything in the fastest way possible. There's a blank version for you in the Appendix.

Pay date	Birthdays & self treats $8/pay	Spare TV $29.10/pay	Coffee table $12/pay	Christmas $20/pay	Spare $6.75/pay
05/04/01	✔	✔	✔	✔	✔ + $3
19/04/01	✔	✔	✔	✔	✔
03/05/01	✔	✔	✔ + $37.30	✔	✔
17/05/01		87.30			
When you		-50.00			
draw up		= $37.30			
your table,		trans. to			
include enough		coffee table			
rows for three					
to six months					
at a time					
Yes, you can					
round your					
figures					
06/09/01					
Approx. cost	$ n/a	$ 350.00	$140.00	$ 520/yr	$ n/a

Tabitha's Goals List (Total savings: $75.85/pay)

Note: $6.75 = $5.85 safety margin from their budget + $0.90 leftover from Tabitha's sanity allowance.

The table becomes easiest to use if your pay gets deposited automatically into your account and:

- If you transfer savings for regular bills into a separate account—which doesn't need to be tracked, by the way, because you've already budgeted how much you need in there over the whole year and:
- If you then take out exactly the same amount every pay for groceries, fuel and loan repayments etc., leaving your sanity allowance, and maybe Christmas and savings for bank fees behind as the only things left to budget.

Any cash change from groceries and other out of pocket expenses stays in your wallet for bonus treats, fresh bread, milk, lotto etc.

Doing this puts practically your entire budget into 'auto-succeed' leaving you with less than $50 a pay to budget strictly.

Yes, I know: the table above says $75.85 a fortnight, not $50, but that's to show you how flexible this system can be. In this case I'm looking at Harley and Tabitha's budget. Harley likes his sanity allowance in his wallet so he can buy a bottle of Scotch every pay, but Tabitha likes to budget hers, so this is her table.

And yes, her sanity allowance is still only $50 a fortnight, but she 'parks' it with their budget's $5.85 'safety margin' and with their Christmas savings for convenience. (She likes to shop for Christmas presents throughout the year whenever she shops for herself so she can take advantage of sales, and so she feels like she's splurging more often than she really is.)

You'll also note an extra $3 adjustment that was deposited into the spare column (someone's sad definition of a back-pay) which was left in there to cover account fees. This particular account didn't have account-keeping fees, but if your savings account does, then this is what you do. You should also: a) consider changing your account and b) don't bother too much fiddling with the balances on this table—just so long as there's always enough in there to cover fees, you won't come to grief if there's a few extra coins unaccounted for.

No, you don't have to wait out the full period to buy everything at the end. As you can see from this example, Tabitha started saving for a spare television set for the family, but after only three fortnights she was able to buy a practically new one from a deceased estate for only $50, so she's amended her columns as shown, transferring the change to her coffee table savings. For the next few pays, she can either save up her $29.10 a pay for something else, or she can share it up amongst her other columns so she's achieving them faster. The choice is hers.

You don't have to budget a whole year at a time with this. In fact you don't have to use the table at all once you get the hang of it. Try for short stints—a few pays at a time—so you get a good feel for your achievements quickly. The whole idea of a sanity allowance, remember, is to reward yourself regularly. So the only reason for saving it up would be to buy bigger things with it than you could ordinarily.

I did use tables religiously for nearly four years—two years before the mortgage, and two years of the mortgage—but that's because they're *sooo* easy to use and I'm slow to break old habits. (Now I keep the tables in my head, although it's not quite as reliable!)

I never saved for any one item longer than six months at a time. And I made the records super-easy to track by keeping the table in my wallet on a slip of paper (with sticky tape around the edges to stop it from tearing) and ticking it off every time I checked my payslip. You'd be surprised how much these wallet tables boost your morale. Try one for yourself and see.

Remember: Unless you're budgeting extremely strictly for a short time, your sanity allowance is IN ADDITION to your purse money (which you get as change from your groceries).

Did you know?

You can manage one account for all your savings for various goals *and* avoid extra account-keeping fees by using the same basic method as described below for budgeting your sanity allowance.

Yes, the record-keeping can be tedious if you have a handful of savings goals and if you achieve them often—otherwise it's a snap.

6

Hot Tips for Big Bucks
Saving Money WITHOUT Cost
Cutting

Big bucks are made up from lots of little bucks, and you can save an awful lot just by being careful HOW you do the things you already do, instead of having to cut back or make compromises in your budget.

MAKING MONEY AND KEEPING IT

To avoid wasting money and to build wealth on a low to middle income while you are still feeling like you're spoiling yourself, simply shift the focus on the kinds of things you buy.

For example, if you buy something that holds (or increases) in value, then you haven't really spent your money after all. You still have it, but it's been transformed into something else. Instead of paper and coins or a bank statement, you'll have land, a house, a reliable secondhand car, furniture or breeding animals, perhaps. These are all tangible things that other people might want, and therefore if you need cash desperately you can sell them.

Suggestions here also include buying gym equipment for home instead of paying 'empty' fees for memberships, or buying electrical goods secondhand or new instead of renting them. Just remember: shop around, buy when on sale if possible, and don't fall for those daytime or late night TV ads.

GIVE YOURSELF A PAYRISE

A penny saved is a penny earned. I don't like that old saying. It completely overlooks modern complications like income tax, stamp duty and GST. So let's modernise it to: *a buck saved is a buck fifty earned*—which is heaps closer to the truth.

As a reality check, remember this the next time you're slogging away at work on overtime or shopping for all your goodies. If your boss won't give you a payrise, or if you feel forced by economic necessity into doing overtime when you'd rather have the time for other things, then score yourself the equivalent of a payrise by shopping cautiously. If you don't have to spend a dollar, then you don't have to earn that extra dollar fifty to pay for it.

GENERAL BUDGET HINTS FOR EVERYONE

- **Never keep money you've kept aside to pay bills at home.** It's a security risk, and it's far too easy for you to dip into for the wrong reasons.
- **Christmas savings:** Failing to save for Christmas is asking for trouble. Even a $200 goal—that's less than $4 a week—can make this expensive time of year a lot more bearable. Open a Christmas goal account—a good hiding hole for holiday savings and kids' pocketmoney too—because you can't usually touch it until Christmas, and there aren't usually any fees. If you can, buy presents well ahead, at sale time, and stash them away carefully until they're needed.
- **For not-so-scary credit card debts up to $2000**, instead of cutting up your card, try freezing it in a cup of water in the back of your freezer—*without closing the account.* This will slow down your usage. You can still make repayments and buy things over the phone of course, just so long as you remember your number.

- **Use trips to McDonald's as rewards** for your children's help around the house, instead of as an expected part of life.
- **Keep a grocery list on the fridge**, write down anything that's running low as soon as you notice it, buy only what's on the list and *never shop when you're hungry*. Chewing on gum usually helps you avoid sweet temptations. Shopping the day before pension day helps you cut down because the shelves are usually the barest, and shopping when you look daggy should make you want to get out of there faster.
- **Budget for credit card interest and bank fees:** Too many people work their budgets out so carefully, but completely forget about interest on credit cards, so they inevitably end up going backwards—despite their efforts.
- **Shop around for car insurance every year or two.** Insurance companies do their maths regularly to figure out which makes and models won the Annual Car Thieves Popularity Contest. As a bonus, owners of winning makes and models win a hike in their premiums.

GST AND THE LITTLE GUY
Get $120 GAS: The GST Assistance Scheme (GAS) is a temporary way for *very* low-income earners to get a once-off $120 bonus, tax free. It's most likely to apply to casual and part-time employees or some uni students. Eligibility is strict. Basically, to get it:

- You can't be receiving any Centrelink payments or be a dependent of anyone else who's getting Centrelink payments;
- AND your assessable income has to be $10,000 or less;
- AND your taxable income has to be $6883 or less;
- AND you have to be an Australian resident (not a new resident);
- AND you have to be over 16 (at 1 July 2000), but you can't be entitled to the Aged Person's Saving Bonus or the Self-Funded Retirees Supplementary Bonus;

HOT TIPS FOR BIG BUCKS   81

- AND you can't be serving a prison sentence.

Check out the full complicated list of cans and can'ts at the Centrelink website: www.centrelink.gov.au or ring them on 13 28 50 to double-check if you're eligible. Then to claim your $120, fill out and submit your Centrelink application form before 30 June 2002.

(Unless extended after this book goes to print, the GAS scheme is only available for the 2000–01 and 2001–02 financial years.)

7

Top Tips for Banking

You can save heaps if you know how to run your chequebook efficiently, use overdrafts effectively, take advantage of netbanking and phonebanking and know about term deposits.

Let's start with my favourite shortcuts on how to balance that dreaded chequebook.

CHEQUEBOOKS
If you're doing personal as opposed to business things with your chequebook you'll only need to tick off all your cheques on your monthly statements to make sure that the amount on your statement equals the amount for which you wrote the cheque. You could do it from memory, but actually ticking them off is proof that you've done it, so you don't do it again later on by accident (and waste your time). When you tick them off, what you're also doing is making sure that they've all been cashed by the dude you gave them to. If they don't get cashed that month, jot a note on your statement of which cheques are missing—and for how much—and deduct the amount from your closing balance so you know how much is really (potentially) in there—just so you don't accidentally spend the money again before all the cheques you've already written are cashed.

Handy tip 1: Put a tick or initial on your cheque butts at the same time as you tick off the correct amounts on the statement so you don't have to get out the previous month's statement each time to check where you were up to—you only have to flip through your chequebook looking for cheque butts that haven't been initialled (or ticked) yet.

Handy tip 2: When you write a cheque, you can skip most of the details on the butt. The only bits you desperately need are 1) the date 2) who it's to 3) what it's for 4) how much. Some people make a major fuss over calculating the new balance in their cheque account each time they write a cheque. There's a spot for this on the butt, but the only time I bother with that is if I'm writing so many cheques at one go that I'm having trouble keeping track of how much is left in there for the next one. So even if I keep a running balance on the bottom of the butts, it's usually rounded to keep the maths quick and easy.

Handy tip 3: When writing a cheque, ask the company to stamp your cheque butt with their company stamp instead of writing out their name in full. (They can stamp the 'made out to' section on the actual cheque too if they like.) You'll not only score all their contact details for future reference, you'll also save time writing the cheque.

Handy tip 4: If you're going to accept a cheque from someone you're nervous about, then try:

1) Asking them for a bank cheque instead of a personal cheque.

2) If they won't give you a bank cheque, ask to see their driver's licence and write the number on the back of the cheque and note this somewhere else—like in your diary— before you bank it. You may need this later to trace and identify them if you eventually need to prosecute them.

3) Try to time collection and payment of the goods so they pay you about five days before your statement is printed. That way you don't have long to wait—or worry—to see if it bounces, and you get out of paying any bank fees to get a fast clearance on it. (Fast clearance fees can be harsh.)

Beware: Bounced cheques are expensive—not to mention annoying—for people at both ends of the cheque, so that's why you need to take five seconds each month to tick off your cheques, as soon as you open the statement envelope. Don't put it off or you won't do it at all. Yes, it's a bit of a pain, but both the writer of the cheque AND the poor sod who tries to cash it get whumped with bounce fees if the cheque does its infamous basketball impersonation—while for the banks in the middle, it's profit city. (If you're on the receiving end, then there's also all the hassle of chasing up a replacement cheque from someone who may have had no intention of paying you in the first place.)

Definition Alert!

A cheque which 'bounces' is also called a rubber cheque. It's one that goes into your account and bounces straight out again—charging you fees for the adventure—because the person who paid it to you is either a crook or having trouble managing their cheque account (sometimes simply because they've underestimated that month's bank fees by as little as one cent). Either way, the cheque is dishonoured by the bank because the person didn't have enough in their account to cover the cheque they gave you. And yes, writing these 'rubbery' cheques is illegal. If you're the one doing it, it will affect your credit rating, even if it is by accident—and it won't affect it in a pleasant way.

What to do if someone gives you a cheque that bounces

a. Contact the person if possible and ask them to arrange cash or a bank cheque immediately, asking them to also pay for the bank fees that you were charged. It's sometimes difficult to get them to pay your bank fees as well, particularly if they feel it's their bank's fault, but you should try.

b. If the person pays for the goods at the time they collect the goods, and if they pay for them with a cheque that bounces, this is fraud. Ring the police if the person in question won't give you the money straight away, or if you can't contact them.

c. If they put the goods on account, or take the goods on the understanding they will pay for them later, and if they eventually pay with a cheque that bounces, then you may need to commence a civil action to get your money or goods back. Contact your local courthouse for details about which court to use (small claims or magistrates) and how to claim. You won't usually need a solicitor as the court will give you all the paperwork you need to process, but it's a lot of hard work for YOU—especially if you didn't do point 2 on page 83!

If you're doing personal and business things within the same chequebook (hobbies count as personal activities), then you've already made a mistake. If you're running a business for which you wish to claim tax deductions (as opposed to an income-producing hobby, which doesn't need records for tax) then you're expected by the Tax Office to keep business accounts and records separate from all of your personal accounts and records.

NIFTY TIPS AND TRICKS FOR USING OTHER BANKING PRODUCTS

OVERDRAFTS

These accounts are operated for the most part like savings accounts, but with the added advantage of being able to go into the red, just like a credit card. Terms and conditions vary from lender to lender, with amounts usually available up to $15,000 without security.

You don't necessarily have to have a business to run an overdraft—private people can have them too. Interest rates on overdrafts are usually lower than for credit cards, personal loans and sometimes car loans; however, overdrafts usually have transaction fees (and government taxes if there's a chequebook attached) which can make them just as expensive as a credit card if you draw money out of them often.

Overdrafts are also similar to personal loans in some ways. They each have standard repayments. But unlike a personal loan, you don't have to explain why you want the money each time. You only pay application fees on an overdraft once at the very beginning—and a rare few credit unions and building societies don't even charge those.

Consider using an overdraft with a debit card if you don't like credit cards, but have regular unexpected expenses of $1000 or more AND if you have the ability to keep up repayments even when you don't owe money on them. If you are in the red, these repayments pay off the debt quickly. If you're in the black, your repayments become regular savings towards your next big expense or goal. Overdrafts therefore make handy bill savings accounts.

Overdrafts are also ideal as investment accounts if you wish to trade in shares. They usually pay high interest when you're in the black, so they're a handy place to park your cash when you sell shares AND borrowing from them helps you buy bargain shares if the opportunity pops up sooner than when you had planned to buy. (Interest on borrowings to buy shares—even in such short-term instances—is tax deductible.)

Note: Overdraft repayments are calculated as if you always owe the full amount, so your debts are kept under fast repayment plans, unlike credit cards which only request a minimum payment if that's all you can afford that month. And yes, you can make extra repayments off overdrafts at any time.

Overdraft tip 1: If you get a credit or debit card linked to your overdraft instead of a chequebook, you can often cut down on transaction fees.

Overdraft tip 2: Try using your overdraft as a bill savings account, so it's only in the red when all your bills bomb your mailbox at once. If you pay all your bills on a credit card—perhaps one that has a loyalty scheme—and pay your credit card on its due date out of the overdraft, then you'll get the benefit of a no interest-free period, a loyalty scheme, lower interest rates and only one transaction a month on your over-draft—the best of all worlds.

TERM DEPOSITS

Usually, the longer you lock your money in a term deposit, the greater the interest rate you earn; but interest may be credited only quarterly or worse, instead of monthly, as for shorter term deposits.

Term deposit tip 1: Save time chasing the best rates by checking financial papers in the back near the stockmarket reports for the best-paying term deposit rates.

Term deposit tip 2: Interest rates are offered on 'bandwidths' of deposits—eg. 6% may be the going rate for deposits between $1000 and $10,000; 6.1% for $10,001 to $50,000; and so on. They can also be offered at higher interest rates for longer terms, but occasionally you may be able to deposit into short-term accounts for the same—or very close to—rates as for long-term deposits. If this is the case, then consider splitting your money into smaller deposits that roll over more regularly to 'trick' the bank's computers into paying you more interest—and with the ability to cash a portion of your investment without penalty, instead of locking in the whole amount for the full term. For instance—using the bandwidth previously mentioned—if you have $10,000 to invest with the choice of investing it at 6% for two months or 6% for 12 months, then try splitting it into ten $1000 deposits which roll over every two months. Tick the box on your application forms to ensure your interest rolls in with your principal for another two-monthly term and you'll effectively turn your simple interest into compounding interest—earning you an extra 0.15% in this case for the year. It's only about $15 extra in this case, but it's still about half a tank's worth of fuel and better in your pocket than anyone else's—especially since you also get better access to your money with lower penalties.

PHONEBANKING AND BPAY

By using a pin number and following instructions over the phone, you can find out loan and savings balances, transfer money between accounts, double-check recent transactions and pay many bills if the company you are paying has a BPAY biller code. (BPAY biller codes are provided in the payment options on the back of your bill.) Beware of BPAY fees. Ask your bank how they permit you to avoid them.

Phonebanking does everything that netbanking does— except with a voice in your ear instead of a screen in front of your face—and is the cost of a local call.

NETBANKING

It's the way of the future, we're told, because—for the banks— it will be easier and cheaper for us to access our funds than for them to provide us with branches and staffing to tend to our inquiries. But with a cost of about $2000 for a suitable PC every few years and ongoing internet, power and phone charges of about $350 a year, it's definitely not cheaper for us, unless we have other convenient or profitable uses for our PC. This means that a lot of the people who can least afford bank fees, including pensioners and people on very low incomes, are the ones being disadvantaged by the push to netbanking.

But if you are one of the computer-fortunate, then netbanking can be a little more enjoyable than phonebanking, except you don't have a computer voice in your ear to alert you to any mistakes.

The security of your electronic information isn't as much of a problem as it's sometimes hyped up to be anymore. Sure, there's still a risk that your credit card details can be hacked and thieves can use it for a spending spree, but you have that risk—albeit to a lesser degree—whether you use netbanking or not. As long as you keep an eye on your records and report any problems straight away, retailers are usually at a greater risk of losing money than you are.

8

How to House-train your Credit Card and Get a Credit Rating Better Than Some Countries

CHOOSING TO LIVE WITH THE DEMON

There's always been arguments for and against having a credit card—in the end, the decision comes down to personal choice. But if you do have one, the chances are that there are quite a few tricks you don't know about that will turn the potential demon that so many fear into your obedient slave.

Believe it or not, having a credit card can help you to financial success if you start off on a low income.

Sadly, many people—not only on low incomes—have landed themselves in boiling financial water using credit cards, mainly because they spend the maximum allowed and repay the minimum allowed. You only have to think about that for a moment and you realise how brain-warped that is. But the credit card limit and the minimum amount required that month are the two loudest numbers that people notice on their credit card statements and it's all too easy to forget everything else.

Please do not let your decision to avoid credit cards be based on fear of becoming one of these financially lost souls. If you set rules for your credit card, and only use your credit card for set purposes—like paying bills over the phone and then paying your credit card with one withdrawal from your bill savings account—then you can actually get some seriously good bonuses.

Each lender has slightly different advantages, but the most common of these include varying degrees of:

- Loyalty scheme points for each dollar spent, which you can convert into discounts and free vouchers on useful things (like fuel, whitegoods or groceries).
- A fair guarantee of getting what you order over the phone or internet—or your money back, even if the company has gone bust.
- Insurance if goods ordered and paid for by credit card arrive damaged.

Also, since some companies permit you to pay a 30-day store account with credit cards, you can sometimes buy things on account, then put off paying the account until the due date. Then, if you pay with a credit card that has a 55-day interest-free period, you can practically turn your 30-day deadline to pay into an 85-day interest-free deadline. This can almost double the time you have to save up to pay for the unexpected expense you put on your store account (like car repairs or a replacement refrigerator). But don't make this a habit or you'll be stepping onto a debt roundabout. The idea is to get debt-free in the fastest, cheapest way possible.

> **Note: You can't pay one credit card with another credit card, but you can pay some store accounts with credit.**

Rule 1 to surviving life with a credit card—if you're at all concerned about lacking the discipline to avoid impulse buys, never carry it with you when you go out. That way you can't use it for impulse buys. Combine it with the rule of never putting anything on layby—which is actually more dangerous as far as impulse buying is concerned—and make sure you never carry more than $20 in your wallet and you're practically guaranteed to avoid impulse buying.

Rule 2 to surviving life with a credit card is to never look at the minimum repayment figure—don't even glance at it—as this may barely be enough to cover interest if you're nearing your credit limit. Look instead at the total balance owing and use as much of your spare budget and bill paying account as you can to pay out as much of it as you can.

Note: Once you are financially successful and you've got the hang of this, you may actually find it beneficial to occasionally OVERPAY your credit card—like I do—making room for extremely big purchases on a credit card with only a small limit. If you haven't guessed, this earns you stacks more loyalty points, which in turn earn you more freebies.

Overpay your credit card a few times and rarely—if ever—miss paying your statement in full by the due date, and your credit rating will be so good entire nations will be jealous.

MINIMUM REPAYMENTS

The lenders do desire a minimum repayment, but that's because many people—myself included sometimes—would forget or neglect to pay at all, if we didn't HAVE to pay something. So in that respect, a minimum repayment is good for us.

Why should you never just pay the minimum?

Let's say interest rates are 16% a year, and the monthly minimum repayment is 1.7% of the balance (with a minimum of $25). Every time you make only the minimum repayment—and assuming you never miss a repayment—you are only paying off your debt by an average of 0.36% a month!

On $2000, that's only getting you ahead about $7 to $9 a month LESS government taxes and other charges. And at that rate, it will take you 23 years to pay it off—and that's assuming you never put another thing on credit!

It would be even better for us from a budgeting point of view if the minimum repayment was at least double what it usually is, because at least then we would—ever so slowly—be paying it off, instead of just coping with monthly fees and charges.

If you're getting a credit card for the first time, there are certain things you should look for. And even if you already have a credit card it's a good idea to stop and consider whether the one you have is the right one for you.

Choose a credit card with an interest-free period if you are likely to be able to make repayments in full at least twice a year. Otherwise, you will probably be better off with the credit card that charges interest straight away on every day's balance owing. These cards have a higher rate of interest, but are by far the cheapest to operate if you can pay them out in full on their due dates regularly—which of course is what you'd do if your bill savings account has been budgeted correctly.

Choose a credit card with no interest-free period— that's one that charges interest on every single day's balance (but the interest is about 2% cheaper):

- If you can't usually keep up with repaying the full statement in total.
- If your credit card is empty for most of the year, then fills up when all your bills bomb your mailbox at once and it takes you months to pay it off again.

Loyalty programs: Who but a bank could come up with the idea of paying to be loyal? Joking aside, you do need to be wary of loyalty programs which have a joining or annual fee. Ask yourself what possible benefit you could get out of paying to be loyal, when there are loyalty programs which ask for nothing except your patronage to their good product and customer service. Work out if the benefits exceed the fees.

To compare schemes follow these simple steps:

1. Look back at your budget and total all your groceries, bills and other expenses per fortnight which you can pay either in person or over the phone using your credit card.
2. Multiply this fortnightly amount by 26 to get the maximum

amount you are likely to pay on credit in any one year. (Or multiply it by 52 if your expenses are calculated weekly.)

3. Convert this amount into points. For example, the Commonwealth Bank True Awards Scheme converts every one dollar into one point, so $5000 spent a year equals 5000 points (not counting bonus points).

4. Now look at the specific rewards offered. Ask for the latest list of points required for those offers and a sample brochure.

WHICH CREDIT CARD?

The following is a quick comparison guide for credit cards offered by a small sample of financial institutions (listed alphabetically). I've included a column for contact phone numbers so you can check if details are correct when it's time for you to choose.

Please note that inclusion in this table is by no means a recommendation of any of these financial products in particular. There may indeed be better offers available by the time you read this, so I've included space at the bottom of this table for you to fill in details for any other bank, building society or credit union with which you may prefer to compare when the time comes. The table is intended as a guide to the sorts of things you should ask about.

Don't be deceived. You may be required to start a savings account in order to get a credit card application approved with a particular bank. But you are rarely obliged to keep it open for long. If you want a particular bank's credit card and you're required to start a savings account first, but you'd rather use $5 notes as toilet paper than change your existing banking habits, then consider using the new bank account as a Christmas saver or furniture goal account for a little while. That way you can satisfy the bank's request for you to deposit to the account regularly, and it will be quick and easy for you to simply close the account when you spend the money in a few months' time.

Quick comparison credit card guide

Note: Bankcards are accepted in Australia only. Mastercards and Visa are accepted worldwide, as is the relatively new Amex credit card. (Rates are current at May 2001.)

Bank	Phone	Annual Fee	%	Up to 55-days interest free?	Loyalty program	Notes
ANZ (sample only)	131314					ANZ has about 20 different credit cards that can be used in more than one way each. Compare them all online at www.anz.com
Bankcard		$26	16.75	Yes	Qantas/Telstra Visa Scheme earns points to spend on phone bills or flights	
Qantas/TelstraVisaGold		$100	17.75	Yes		
Visa standby		$22–$26	12.25	No		
Commonwealth Bank	132221					
All cards have three choices:						Offers Bankcard, Mastercard & Visa
option 1:		$45	16.65	Yes	True Awards Program	
option 2:		$24	16.65	Yes	No True Awards	
option 3:		Nil	14.75	No	No True Awards	
Virgin Money Mastercard	1800 080 000	Nil	11.9	No	Yes	Introductory interest rate of 4.9% for first six months.
National Bank	132265					Cash advance fees are $1 to $1.50. Note: Interest-free is only 44 days instead of 55 days on all cards
Bankcard		$18	16.25	Yes	Fly buys can be linked to all cards	
Mastercard		$26.40	16.25	Yes	Gold Card Rewards:	
Visa		$26.40	16.25	Yes	Qantas Frequent Flyers	
Gold Mastercard		$88.30	16.25	Yes		
Gold Visa		$88.30	16.25	Yes		
Your choice of credit union/ building society						

FATAL MISTAKE: FAILING TO BUDGET FOR CREDIT CARD INTEREST

Did you realise how much of your credit card repayments are eaten by interest? I know that putting all your income—or as much as you can—into your credit card seems like a warped and scary thing to do. And actually encouraging you to buy things on credit seems completely whacked out, since that's what got you into trouble in the first place. But until you get on top of it—and to save stacks on interest as described in the radical credit card attack on page 96—try banking as much of your income as you can straight into your credit card, practically everything except your wallet money and sanity allowance, until it's time to spend it. If you put your cash where you're afraid to use it—where it's harder to get at, and where you have to sign for it to get it out—then you will be forced to find ways around spending it. You'll be amazed at just how inventive you can be sometimes to avoid the hassle of spending! Just make sure you stick to your budget so you always spend at least $100 less than the income you deposit to your card each pay. Soon, all your spare money will be 'sitting' in your credit card, waiting for the next bill to come in.

THE DIFFERENCE BETWEEN CREDIT CARDS AND DEBIT CARDS

A debit card can only be used to spend money that you already have in your savings or cheque account, depending on which one it is linked to. EFTPOS fees apply to debit cards, however some banks give you plenty of free transactions per month if you also have a mortgage or term deposit with them.

A credit card, however, puts you in debt to the bank by the amount of your purchase or cash advance PLUS interest (depending on whether an interest-free period), PLUS the annual fee (sometimes charged regularly). Negligible government taxes (usually less than $1 per month) may also apply. If you get slugged with any other bank fees or charges, you're probably on a raw deal—shop around for a new credit card.

Credit cards can be used exactly the same as debit cards—only without the hefty EFTPOS fees—especially if you keep your credit card 'overpaid' just like a savings account. The only drawback on being overpaid may be that bank computers aren't used to this unusual occurrence and if you ring to find out what your balance is, you may be told by the computer voice that you owe $230 when in fact the bank owes you that much. It's a glitch, but it's a glitch we can live with while EFTPOS fees are so outrageous.

Also, since interest paid to you on your debit card accounts is usually embarrassingly pathetic, you're not missing much, even if you do choose to go with a credit card that doesn't pay interest to you if you overpay it.

RADICAL CREDIT CARD ATTACK

Note: The following 'package' solution is intended for people with serious *existing* credit debts by providing them with a number of advantages, the main one being to keep down the interest charges. If you feel confident that you're in control of your spending, just pick the bits that interest you and adapt them to suit individual circumstances.

Trick 1: A loophole. Few people realise you can actually go into 'the black' with your credit card by overpaying the balance owing as mentioned above. (One Visa card—an ANZ Visa card—even pays you interest if it happens!) It's a pretty funny idea actually: *the bank owing you money* on your credit card! But because of pathetic interest rates and bank fees on savings accounts, it's a loophole worth exploiting for really serious credit card debts.

Because interest is calculated daily, if you deposit as much of your income in it as you can, you're 'tricking' the computer into calculating interest on a much smaller amount every day. (I wish I could copyright that idea!) Your income will 'sit' in your credit card until you need it, saving you money every single day. On a full credit card with a $2000 limit, that's saving about $25 a month.

And there are no EFTPOS fees!!!

If you decide to deposit your *entire* pay to your credit card, then either: a) keep aside your $15 to $40 a fortnight flash cash—depending on how much you worked out you could afford in chapter 4: Lazy Budgeting, or b) get a cash advance for your pocket expenses—but note a warning: regardless of what type of credit card you have, you pay interest on cash advances right away anyhow.

After setting this up to deposit automatically, stick to your new budget. Live by the motto, 'If it's not budgeted for, then you can't have it.' And with the exception of bills that you've budgeted for, never spend more than you deposit each pay.

It might be a scary way of attacking a credit card bill—especially when that's what got you into trouble in the first place. But it's a great shortcut if you're careful.

Did you know?

Keeping only one card in the family—and keeping it in the name of the person who hates shopping most—will also force you to curb spending because you'll have to shop together, where both of you can see what the other is up to.

If you're already scared of using credit cards, then this radical attack can be even more beneficial because some places won't EFTPOS extra cash available out on credit cards anymore, so you'll HAVE to be more careful with the cash in your pocket.

Trick 2: Paying credit with credit (once only!) There's only one time you can legally pay credit with credit: when you're opening one account to close another. The terms and conditions vary slightly in the fine print between banks, but generally, the card with an interest-free period charges about 2% higher interest rates than the one that starts charging interest straight away. Therefore, if your spending habits and balance owing fluctuate greatly throughout the year then it might not matter much which method you choose.

But if you're the type of person who can pay their credit card off in full—and on time—at the end of each month, then as mentioned earlier, you'll usually do better with a credit card that has an interest-free period.

If, on the other hand, you're the type that gets yourself into debt and then tries to pay it off somehow—while continuing to buy things on credit—then you'll be better off with the card that charges a lower rate of interest, but charges it straight away. But in taking this second option of a permanently interest-charging card, you're practically accepting that you're likely to be in debt for the rest of your life, and are hoping to make it as painless as possible.

The only way I can think of to ease the pain of it is to use trick 1 above: depositing your pay to your credit card to 'trick' the bank's computer into calculating less interest. And the truth is, on a $2000 limit, the best it can do is save you about $40 a year.

But if you switch cards you can get a little bit further ahead.

By changing from a card with one interest scheme to a different kind, you can apply to have your new credit card pay out your old credit card—even if they're with different banks. Do this by ticking the appropriate box on your application form when you apply for your new card (make sure you ask them to cancel your old credit card in the process).

If you're changing to a credit card which also has a loyalty scheme, then you'll also pick up a whack of loyalty points (discounts to the value of the balance owing on your old card when you pay it out).

Trick 3: If you change from a 'no free period' card to a 'free period' card then you can have up to $80 a year extra (for every $2000 owing) to pay on the 'free period' card because of its higher interest rate. **But only** if you slack off on your budget and allow your credit card to remain full for most of the year. Remember, **you do** get an interest-free period, which saves you up to $86 in one hit (on a $2000 debt). So even if you're a little naughty, you still should come out in front with the more expensive 'free period' card.

Trick 4: Budget bonuses. Loyalty scheme points could traditionally be redeemed for holiday and funpark discounts or an exemption from the annual card fee. But as more companies discover the marketing advantage to supporting these schemes, credit card users are finding they can now also redeem their points for everyday consumables including fuel, groceries, furniture, household whitegoods, alcohol and video hire—all of which provide a worthwhile bonus for any household budget.

For example, an average family of four could easily spend $230 per fortnight on groceries and $60 on fuel. Put these on credit instead of paying by EFTPOS and you not only dodge fees, you also pick up 7540 points a year which is enough to redeem for $50 worth of fuel on the Commonwealth Bank Mastercard. Pay your bills and other expenses on credit in order to withdraw money from your savings account only twice a month (once for cash for your pocket and once to pay your credit card) and you can be earning up to 30,000 points a year with very little effort at all.

9

A Roof over your Head

As I mentioned earlier, in Lazy Budgeting that Does Everything Except the Dishes, sharing your living expenses with friends, relatives—and even a few flatmates that you only just met through the classifieds—can be very tempting indeed when you're finding it tough to survive on your own.

Sadly, statistics show that the majority of people who try to casually blend relationships with personal finances—especially where those relationships are not genuine unions of hearts, souls and wallets and where the rules aren't set upfront—have a slim chance of survival at best.

But household expenses and grocery bills only know one direction—and it's not down. Which makes the idea of sharing your life, assets, income and living expenses with your best mate and their toenail clippings, empty beer bottles and dirty washing, seem like an almost bearable concept at times.

So what can you do?

PART A: OPTIONS FOR PEOPLE RENTING OR BUYING

Firstly, interview potential flatmates carefully. You need to be reasonably sure they're not hatchet murderers and that you can live together without driving each other insane, but you also want to get a feel for the more common points of aggravation, many of which centre on money and belongings. And remember, you are interviewing them, but they should also be interviewing you.

Hotspots often involve: sharing or unauthorised use of personal toiletries, towels, Tim Tams, alcohol and telephones. Head these off by setting rules in advance and making sure everyone has at least one area to call their own personal space. (For example, set aside some shelves or cupboards for each person.)

Try returning the phone to the landlord for safekeeping so there are no arguments over who ran up the $500 in calls to a clairvoyant. Or call Telstra and organise a 'phone bar'— ensuring this is approved by the landlord if necessary—which means you can receive calls from anyone, but you can only ring out to emergency numbers and Telstra assistance lines. You can also get special handsets with PIN numbers for each tenant, but this relies on tight security of PINs. However, if you mainly receive calls instead of making them, consider using personal mobile phones as an alternative to a single house phone, as this can be cheaper, depending on your usage.

Many joint tenants have a leading tenant, usually the person who's lived there first—or the longest—who ensures the rent gets paid, that new tenants are advertised for, interviewed and selected. Sometimes the leading tenant may actually be the owner who may be taking in boarders in order to afford repayments to their own home if they've fallen on hard times. (I've known people who've been unable to keep up repayments after interest rate rises, so they sell their homes to an investor to get back whatever cash they can, on the understanding that they can stay on as a tenant with a right to sub-let if they choose.) To avoid arguments over money, work out and agree to your budget and chores as a group—even if there is a 'boss tenant'.

To avoid running out of anything, keep a standard shopping list of everything that gets bought every week stuck to the fridge. Create it as a simple form and print it off or photocopy it so you don't have to write it out each time. Add to this every time somebody finishes something that's not a regular weekly purchase. That way, if you're unable to organise a mutually agreeable time to shop together or if you decide to make it a rostered chore, the people who do shop have a very good idea of what to buy—no matter how long they may have been living together. This list will appear long by comparison to some handwritten shopping list scrawls, but we're aiming for speed, ease, convenience and most importantly, consensus. You probably won't have to do it for long—just until you get used to living together.

In addition to the groceries list, work out right from the start who will be doing the cooking, the toilet-scrubbing, the rent-paying and anything else that might need doing.

Handy hint: **Keep receipts and return non-perishables the next week if they were bought by accident or are not likely to be used. Do it during your next shopping trip so you don't waste time or fuel.**

PART B: FOR PEOPLE BUYING THEIR HOMES

I meet so many people these days who don't think they can afford a house of their own so they commit to sharing the purchase of a house with their brothers or sisters or best mates, so everyone has a roof over their heads.

As tempting as this may sound, it's just asking for trouble. Arguments over maintenance and running expenses, style, colours and landscaping are too easy to fall into. Complications like marriage, divorce, job transfer to another region or unexpected children can also upset your long-term commitments to each other. Eventually, someone will want out of the arrangement and if you can't afford to buy them out you're going to have to sell up too. (Just getting a valuation to keep everyone happy for the buyout is a good trick by itself.)

You have other options:

If one parent (often Mum) can't afford to keep the family home after the other parent has passed away, either:

a) Let them move in with you at no charge, but claim them as a dependent for tax purposes if you're supporting them ($22–$60 per fortnight) and also—if they're unable to look after themselves—apply for the Centrelink Carer's Payment if applicable ($390 approx. if you're single or $330 approx. each for you and your spouse PLUS $82 if they're living with you.) You will, however, need to gently assert that the house rules are your own now and not the ones you grew up with.

b) Instead of sharing ownership and mortgage repayments, perhaps the parent concerned could buy your car off you? Of course, you'll still be the one to use it to get you both around. But at least when your surviving parent does pass away, you should only be arguing with your brothers and sisters over a car—and not your house.

Or if it's friends or other family that can't be claimed as dependents, either:

a) If they're on a pension, rent them a room for the equivalent of the 'rental assistance' portion of their pension. If they're going to pay rent, it might as well benefit someone they know. But remember that you can't negative-gear any portion of your own home even if you rent part of it.

Warning: If you're mixing friends or family with home ownership, always try to keep your finances as 'clean cut' as possible with clear rules and establish consistent habits over who pays for what and why. Otherwise—if things turn nasty—you could lose out terribly in a 'custody battle' over your house.

PART C: IF YOU'RE STILL LIVING AT HOME

Living at home and having your parents provide or subsidise your existence is definitely a cheap way to start out on the right foot in life. But I'm going to suggest something—in the interests of teaching you independence—that will threaten your concept of Nirvana.

Yes, shock, horror: I'm suggesting you pay your parents a contribution towards housekeeping expenses even if they haven't already asked you to ($5 a week if you're unemployed, up to $50 a week if you're employed with a decent job).

Pay to live with my own family!? Are you crazy?

Probably. I must admit the idea didn't boot my PC much at first either. But as unappealing as paying your parents may seem at first, it's the cheapest and fastest route to independent financial success. Don't think of it as buying their love, or paying them to keep caring for you. Think of it as your first profitable business negotiation in a *relatively*—pardon the pun—safe environment.

Try to get in first—timing your approach to coincide with their good moods—because leaving your parents to bring up the subject could result in them plucking a weekly or fortnightly figure for you out of thin air. And it's often whatever their workmates reckon is a fair thing, rather than being based on a sound financial calculation that is harmonious with your goals.

Sit down with your parents—your whole family, if that's what it takes—and work out a deal where you can stay for one or two more years (depending on your income), and you will probably discover that your parents are only too keen to help you out.

When it comes down to it, your parents have already spent at least 17 or so years and tens of thousands of dollars getting you through school and maybe university, so it makes next to no sense at all to stop subsidising you now, when they are so close to achieving their goal of producing an independent, well-organised adult.

Your parents might even surprise you

I paid $30 every fortnight for four years to Mum for housekeeping.

Then she spent the whole $3000 on presents for me for my 21st birthday—when I had planned to move out.

So in the end, I got it all back again anyway . . . with her blessings!

See also page 19 'Buying a house: how to get it.'

10

Wheels for Work and Play

There are so many ways to get stuck with a lemon these days, I couldn't fit them all into one chapter, but in this section I hope to alert you to the most common lurking dangers that face you when it's time to get mobile, and show you how to avoid them.

I've also included a sample car loan application—with tips on how to sign safer contracts of any kind—as well as providing details, tricks and tips for your financing options, including some that may seem a bit radical but work well if they suit your personal circumstances.

CHOOSING YOUR CAR

Beware of the difference between cost and price! Price is what the car is advertised for. Cost is the initial price, the interest and the emotional and lifestyle complications that go with it. For example, the sale price of a brand new car might be $18,000, but over five years of repayments at current rates it's more likely to cost you $24,000 to $28,000. That extra six to ten grand in interest goes a long way towards a deposit on a flat or house.

Choice time: Do you really want to let yourself slip behind financially so fast? You don't have to. You have plenty of options.

Public transport is the first alternative if it's not too incon-
venient AND if it's cheaper than petrol and parking and other
running costs. You can always hire an economy car for weekends or trips away.

If it's your first car and you're just starting out in life and
your parents are in a financial position to make you a loan,
then that's an option too. But only consider it if you have
an excellent relationship with them and they're not the type
to try to hold power over you because of it. At worse, they
can keep an intrusive eye on your mileage, or set rules over
when or if you're allowed to drive it. And if it's registered
in their names, they can sell it out from under you at any time,
or drive it whenever they wish at your expense. On the other
hand, even if your relationship is great, you can still feel guilty
if you know that by helping you out, they're putting a strain
on their finances. And it can be embarrassing if the car's
registered in their names when you're naughty behind the
wheel, because parking fines and speeding tickets will get issued
to them.

The final alternative is paying for your own wheels. If cheap,
convenient public transport isn't an option, it's the only way to
get independence and job flexibility. For tips and tricks on how
to do this, read on.

A WORD ON HOTRODS AND LEAD FOOTS . . .

Okay—guys especially—if you're under 25, get your eyes off
that hotrod. On top of initial purchase and repair costs, you'll
have dearer insurance and possibly registration. But even if you
can afford to buy it now, as well as fix it and keep it going, your
budget is unlikely to appreciate the ongoing attention you'll
get from your local constabulary. Fact 1: blue uniforms are
attracted to smoking rubber because of Fact 2: adolescent
males who drive hot fixer-uppers are statistically more likely to
have lead in their feet and booze in their blood.

Traffic fines are pointless budget blow-outs. Avoid them
wherever possible.

HUNTING THE MARKET WITHOUT GETTING SKINNED

Choosing which type of car you want is entirely up to you, but there are a number of things on which you can base your decision. Namely: price, size, fuel economy, long-term reliability, simplicity or economy of repairs and maintenance, safety, level of comfort, whether it's air-conditioned or not, colour, and preferred manufacturer—not necessarily in that order, and you certainly don't have to be limited to these options.

For each of these points there are countless tricks on how to get a better or safer deal, so here's at least one trick for each of these points. Hopefully they will save you money. They should also inspire you to think of new tricks of your own.

Trick 1: If you wish to base your decision on price AND if the car is secondhand through a dealer, then compare prices carefully with prices that are available from private sellers for similar cars—check your local daily newspaper or trading post-style paper (these are usually weekly newspapers), or check out a magazine from your newsagent which specialises in cars for sale. If you're in a trade union, then also ring your union shopper and ask their car-finders to locate the best price they can find on the vehicle of your choice. And ring Telstra's 131SHOP for the cost of a local call for the contact details of three dealers in your area who may be able to hunt this up for you, as well as three 'car-finder companies' which operate in your state. You'll have to provide each of these organisations with your desired make, model, year range, desired accessories, colour preferences and price bracket, and in return they'll search their traders' network for a match and contact you. (Avoid car finder companies which are not free of charge.)

Trick 2: When trying to choose make or model, try going for test drives through two different dealerships and getting written quotes from both—even if they sell the same make of cars—because their salespeople will nearly always point out different selling features of the car according to their level of knowledge.

> ## Useful websites when buying or selling a vehicle:
>
> For listings of classic and prestige cars for sale or wanted in Australia try:
>
> ### www.finder.com.au
>
> For easy new or used car searches in Australia and for valuations on your existing car, try:
>
> ### www.carsales.com.au
> ### or www.drive.com.au

Beware the sales pitch

Salespeople are there to get the best price they can for their secondhand cars. They're also obligated by legislation to present cars for sale only if they're roadworthy, so if the car looks a bit dodgy on the following roadworthy tips, then it's likely that the salesyard is at worst a mob of crooks, and at best, operating unprofessionally. Either way, if they refuse to allow you to take the vehicle to a mechanic of YOUR choice for a pre-purchase check, turn your back and walk away from trouble.

Note: Pre-purchase checks cost anywhere from $40 to $120 but you get a written report which can save you thousands in potential repairs. Yes, you can ask the seller to fix everything on the list before you buy it, but they may not agree. And since you paid for the check you may be handing them the information they need—for free—that may help them figure out what to bodgy up before the next poor schmuck comes along. Instead—if you're still interested—try negotiating that the sale will be conditional upon the car being made roadworthy with any costs deducted from the purchase price.

A car will fail a roadworthy—also called a safety

certificate or pink slip, depending on your state—for many reasons. Some you may not have thought about are: sunken seats; frayed seatbelts; cracked or damaged windscreens in the driver's line of sight; steering wheels with bits missing in the vinyl; anything not working, even on the dash; gear lever loose; peeled or bubbled window tinting. Also, the driving lights need to be fitted so they're wired independently so you can switch them on and off independently but they can't come on with low beam, only high beam. Fan belts and hoses should not be perished. And yes . . . a safety (roadworthy) certificate does mean that the car must be in mechanically working order at the time you buy it.

Scoping you out: Salespeople take their time to try to assess if you know what you're talking about, to see if you're an easy mark for selling you the dog car of the lot or something else that hasn't shifted for a few months. They'll start by asking what you're looking for. The first mistake you make is by answering generally. DO NOT SAY that you're just looking for a reliable car to get you to work, or maybe to get you around town and to the coast on weekends—any car should do this. Read through a car sales magazine and get a general idea of what each model is worth. Then give them specific makes and models that you're interested in, stating what it is that you like about it. Eg. 'I'm looking for a Toyota Camry, because I like the handling and visibility.' Or maybe tell them you've looked at a '98 Holden Commodore and you're just looking to see if there's anything better around before you buy. If they suspect you're vulnerable—and if you wear a skirt like me, many salespeople seem to assume it—they'll try to take advantage of you if they can. *Note:* The lot's lemon will rarely have a price ticket on it. True, many good cars are also un-ticketed, but if advertised at what it's really worth they'd never be able to sell the lemon.

Expect the car yard to be slightly dearer than a private seller—they have to pay wages, rent and advertising, as well as provide some degree of warranty and pay to have the vehicle presented in a fashion that's fit to pass a safety certificate. Always give yourself a cooling down period of a day or two before signing anything and never give deposits without getting a receipt.

THINGS TO LOOK FOR IN SECONDHAND CARS

At $40 to $120 each you can't afford to pay for pre-purchase checks on every car you look at, so you need to be able to eliminate the most obvious lemons before they sour your taste for car shopping. Here's a few guidelines—taught to me by some of the nicest mechanics in the world.

Don't buy the first car you see—and don't use the quality of the sound system as your primary choice of vehicle. Look for these problems instead and shop around, getting a feel for the market first through newspaper ads. (If any of these answers below are a 'yes', then it's probably trouble.)

Points to check	Yes/ No	What it probably means if the answer is yes
General condition:		
• Is the engine covered in oil?		• Oil leaks present.
• Are belts perished or swollen?		• Belts need replacing.
• If it's an old car, is the engine so clean that it's sparkling under the bonnet?		• Oil leaks have been deliberately removed.
Bodywork:		
• Is any paint rippled or not completely smooth? (Use a fridge magnet—of the flexible magnetic business card kind—to detect bog, usually most common near the under edge and corners of the body. Magnets won't stick to bog.		• Rust may have been removed and the panel bogged up.

- Is there lots of rust underneath the door near the two drain holes?
- Is there rust underneath in the chassis or the subframes or the door sills (sills are on body underneath the doors) or under the vinyl/plastic/rubber door trims?

- The doors have had it.

- Rust will need to be cut out

Fresh paint:
- Is there any on the body? (If it's been resprayed, why?)
- Is there any black paint on the chassis underneath?

- Fresh paint anywhere may be trying to hide something. Look closely.

Starting the car with the bonnet up:
- Allow to run until warm. Are there any oil leaks?
- Take off the oil filler cap. Are there fumes?
- Undo the radiator cap—take any jewellery off your hands first for safety—and feel up inside the roof of the radiator's top tank. Is it sludgy?

- Warm oil is thinner and leaks more easily.
- The rings are worn out.

- Grey sludge = blown head gasket or water in the oil. Black and slimy sludge = either engine oil has been in the water from a blown-piston, or the oil gallery plug is leaking, or oil has been forced into the cooling system by a pinhole in either the cylinder head or the gasket.

(*Note*: If the car is ten years old or more, then evidence of a small amount of oil leakage around the engine that's a bit dusty is actually comforting. It means there's been no attempt to hide it.)

Any kind of sludge in your radiator = costly repairs. For example, a late model car with an aluminium overhead cam-shaft fuel injected motor can be about $650 to $1500 to repair.

Dipstick: Oil should be a nice clean 'oily' colour. If whitish, water is present. Seal may be gone

- If it's not, water is present because seals may be gone.

Side of the engine block: Any leaks or dripping?

- Welsh plugs may be leaking.

Under the body:
- Is there any rust, fresh black paint, new welds or freshly ground metal?
- Are there any holes where bolts may have been?

- Repairs have been made.

- Clamps or other pieces may be missing.

Wheels: Look on inside of wheels and under chassis.
- Is there an oily wetness around wheel assemblies?
- If the car is front-wheel drive, check grease boots which are filled with black lithium grease. Are they split?

- Brake fluid or diff oil may be leaking.
- Dirt may get in, creating a grinding paste which wears out the constant velocity joints affecting driving and steering.

On the test drive:
- Are the seats firmly fixed to the floor?
- If the car is a manual, shift into neutral while driving at different speeds. Is there a noise in the back?
- If the car is front-wheel drive, is there a *clock clock clock* sound when turning?
- Maintain light feel on the brakes. Does the brake pedal creep down by itself?

- May be wear in bolts or rust in floor.
- Rear axle bearings are probably shot.

- Grease boots are spilt or constant velocity joints are worn.
- Master cylinder is probably cactus, with fluid leaking.

Technical Advice Courtesy: Betaray Training Academy, Qld.

Beware: Oil and radiator leaks can be 'plugged' for a short time by adding thickeners like 'stop leak' products to hide leaks from buyers. Some additives will also prevent smoke emissions and you won't notice leaks until you change the oil—after you've bought the car. Sadly, there's not much you can do about this except ask, and hope for an honest reply, because you can't usually see, smell or feel if an additive has been put into the system fluids to hide faults.

Trick 3: If you wish to buy a new car, ask your mechanic— or a business which runs its own fleet or any other large-scale company associated with the car industry—to introduce you to the car sales dealership where they usually purchase their vehicles. They can do this by phoning the dealership and letting them know you're coming, or by faxing them, or writing you a letter of introduction to hand to them, or by loaning you their fleet card. You may get a sizeable discount off the purchase price and they may get paid a bonus for referring you (which they might even offer to split with you).

Trick 4: If you wish to base your decision on which brands are the most reliable over longer periods, contact your mechanic for his or her recommendations on which cars require the cheapest or fewest repairs after ten years of age. Also try contacting the auto club in your state for comparison details.

Trick 5: If you wish to base your decision on safety features, performance and/or accessories, check out the websites for each manufacturer by looking up the manufacturer's name, followed by, com.au. For example, the Toyota website would be found with www.toyota.com.au and Holden would be www.holden.com.au

Trick 6: If you're buying a secondhand car, ask who the existing mechanic is and contact them to confirm what major repairs have been done in the last two years, and which parts are still under warranty. Also ask the mechanic if he or she would be prepared to continue as the vehicle's repairer. If it's a lemon—and if they're reputable mechanics—they'll usually be keen to say no and tell you why.

Trick 7: If it's a new car, negotiate your price on—or just before—the last day of the month, as salespeople and dealerships get manufacturer bonuses based on the number of vehicles sold that month, and yours may be just the sale they need in order to jump to the next bonus level. If this is the case, you could score a nice discount in exchange for your autograph on a contract to buy.

Trick 8: Be honest. After going to two dealerships for test drives—getting written quotes from both—tell one salesperson that you're going to attempt to seek a better price at another dealership and that you will ring when you have their offer price. (You don't have to mention which dealership until you make the call.) Tell them that they should calculate the lowest price they are prepared to offer and/or prepare a list of additional accessories they're prepared to throw in. Make sure they have everything they need ready for that phone call, at which time you intend to make your final decision. Then go to the second dealer and ask for a firm lowest quote for a sale that day, advising them that you will be making a pre-arranged phone call to see if you can get it cheaper elsewhere. Again, you don't have to tell them where that is, unless the other people beat their quote.

Take your mobile phone with you when you visit the second dealership and give each salesperson up to two opportunities to match or better each other's offers, then thank the loser for their time and finalise the sale with the dealership who won. It works by taking the pressure off you and putting it onto the salespeople in a healthy competitive environment but if they don't want to play this game, you've lost nothing by trying. You can walk away if you're not happy and try a third dealer.

Trick 9: Contact REVS (Register of Unencumbered Vehicles)

Don't be intimidated

At one stage recently when I was shopping around to replace both my 14-year-old four-wheel drives with brand new vehicles—at a usually reputable dealership—I was harassed by a particularly pushy salesman.

I asked him what his best price was for cash. He told me, and I advised him that I'd already been quoted $2500 less at another dealership in a nearby town, but since he was local and I'd dealt with the dealership before, I told him I'd give him the chance to match that offer. He went to great lengths to explain how it wasn't possible for a dealership to undercut another dealership and he demanded to know who had given me the cheaper price. I told him I preferred not to tell him this as I didn't want them to get into trouble before I'd bought my car. He suggested point blank that I was lying and dared me to buy the car for the lower price.

So I did—and saved nearly $2500 on that car and $5000 on the next one.

Driving past his dealership in my new cars is always enjoyable. I smile and wave.

or VSR (Vehicle Security Register) in your state and pay the small fee to ensure there's no money owing on the car. If there is, split your cheque to pay the current lender with the balance going to the owner, otherwise you can become responsible for the debt.

USED CAR WARRANTY
- **From a car yard** is either six months or a year, on all parts and labour.
- **From a private seller** can be arranged through motor warranty companies on all electrical, mechanical, parts and labour—usually for six months. Check *Yellow Pages* or car sales magazines for advertisements. Some warranty companies also insure for towing costs up to about $100, as well as accommodation (if trouble strikes away from home) and sometimes car hire if required. Warranty costs range from roughly $160 to about $250 for six months, with some offering options to extend the period. To be eligible for the best rates, you—or the previous owner—need to provide evidence of regular servicing over one or two years or more. The current owner can buy this insurance and use it to promote the sale of their car, and it can be transferred to the new owner for a small fee (around $25). Or you can organise the warranty when you buy the car—if the previous owner provides you with receipts as evidence of the service history.

CAR FINANCE
If you haven't saved up for your first or next car in advance, then there's stacks of options available for you to obtain finance.

Option 1: Get a loan from your parents and offer to pay them the going term deposit or home loan interest rate, or do extra chores or favours in exchange for **zero interest**. *Note:* You can consider this option no matter how old you are, just as your parents should be free to request the same favour of you in future when you become financially successful. *Note:* Paying some form of interest means the arrangement is less likely to end in ugly arguments.

Option 2: Borrow from your life insurance policy if it has this option available. There may be a redraw fee and possibly a request to repay the money—if at all—within a certain time-frame. But you don't always have to provide a reason why you want the money and there should be **no interest** charged because you are effectively getting back money you have already paid them. Some policies let you borrow the money back without having to repay anything, because they can simply reduce your benefit upon retirement etc.

Option 3: Cash advance on a credit card has no application fees and interest starts being charged from the day you withdraw the money. You don't need to provide a reason for the cash advance and *in emergencies* repayments can be as low as your monthly minimum or as high as you wish and there's no deadline for repaying the money. This makes repayments extremely flexible if your income is extremely unreliable. Interest rates are about 13% to 17% but you'll obviously be limited to buying a secondhand car (unless you can make up the difference in another way) because it's hard to get a credit card limit greater than $5000 or $10,000 without an excellent credit

---

NEVER leave any blank answers on loan applications or car purchase contracts or other contracts of any kind—even if the lender or salesperson asks you to. If there is no answer applicable then indicate that by writing it, or striking through that space.

The only space which can be safely left blank is the one space where the account number will go if you're a new member. It can be extremely dangerous and costly—I know from personal experience—to sign an authority saying that the lender can complete any accidental blanks as they see fit. You might find yourself stuck with loan 'features' that you would never normally agree to.

rating to start with. Also, cars bought with a cash advance can be considered to be unfinanced, which means insurance will be cheaper. **Beware:** You must work out how much you need to repay in order to pay off your cash advance in three to eight years—and use discipline to stick to it. Because if you only make minimum repayments without trying to catch up you can end up paying the loan off for the rest of your life—or worse—exceeding the credit card limit and incurring extreme penalties.

Option 4: *A personal loan* will have application fees, may require that you specify the reason for the loan, will have interest rates ranging anywhere from 12% to 25%, fixed terms and penalties for early payout. Personal loans do sometimes allow extra repayments without penalties, but if you go through one of the finance companies at the top end of the interest rate scale there's a greater chance with some of the less reputable or heavy-handed lenders of having large men show up on your doorstep if you're late in making a payment. If the car is provided as security for the loan then its insurance premiums will be higher, usually between $30 and $130 a year, depending on make and model.

Option 5: *An overdraft* has a once-only application fee. It doesn't always require you to nominate a specific reason for the loan if no security is required. It has interest rates around 10% to 15%, but it will also pay you interest if you pay out your loan and start using it as a savings account. You usually get a chequebook or debit card attached to your overdraft, which means you can use it for more than just buying your car so long as you don't go over your overdraft limit. And if you don't have to nominate the reason for the unsecured overdraft, then the car can be considered to be unfinanced, which allows you to get the cheaper insurance premiums.

Option 6: *Car finance*—Interest rate is roughly 10% to 12% but can be as high as 28% with rates varying depending on how much you pay for the car and where you get the loan. Interest rates are usually cheaper if you go through the dealer from whom you buy your car, and if you do buy a car through a dealer, the finance company will usually refer all paperwork through the dealer anyway—even if you apply for the loan directly with the lender—because they need to look after their biggest clients.

Option 7: *Corporate finance/hire purchase*—If you're self-employed or own a company, you can be eligible for corporate finance for hire purchase, which may have an application fee, but has cheaper interest rates, roughly equivalent to home loan rates. You can also negotiate a payout figure, which effectively means that your loan is only for a portion of the car's value. The balance is paid as a lump sum at the end of the loan, at which time you can sell the car and buy a new one to start all over again. For instance, if a car is worth $30,000, you might apply for a five-year loan with a payout figure of $5000 at the end, hoping that you will be able to sell the car for $10,000 which gives you $5000 cash towards the next car.

Note: If the car—or a portion of it—is used for business, you will be able to get tax deductions for interest, fees and charges, no matter what type of loan you get. You'll also be able to claim depreciation on the purchase price—see your accountant for further details.

Tax deduction trick: No matter how you pay for a business car, consider getting the car Scotch-guarded, rust-proofed, sound-proofed, paint-protected and/or window-tinted (if you're that way inclined) AFTER you pick it up. The compelling reason for this is you may be able to save up to 50% on these costs by shopping around for the best price as well as eliminating 'the middle man'—ie. the person who organises this for you at the car sales dealership—by dealing directly with the car detailing company. Also, if these extras are included on the purchase contract and have already been done to the vehicle when you take possession, you'll have to depreciate them with the purchase price. But if you pay for them separately on a later day, you may be able to write them off as expenses in that financial year for a more immediate benefit AND you'll be able to reclaim the GST applicable to those extra expenses in full,

whether it's within the first two years of the introduction of
GST or not.

Some advisers recommend that if you have enough equity in
your home loan, you can often refinance your home loan to a
larger amount, using the extra to pay for your car. If the
combined new loan means that you're borrowing more than
80% of your house valuation, then you'll have to pay extra
insurance on the loan and/or put the new car up for security as
well. Most people who refinance their homes to buy a car do so
because the home loan interest rate is around 6% to 8.5%,
which is cheaper than a personal loan, and minimum repayments are lower than for separate home and personal loans
(because the personal loan is paid out over a much shorter term).

Refinancing trick 1: If you can get away with just using your
house as security and get the money for the car paid into a
savings or cheque account before you pay it to the seller, then
your car can be considered to be fully paid for. Again, unfinanced cars have cheaper insurance.

Refinancing trick 2: If you get your car loan incorporated into
your home loan, make sure you increase your total repayments
by an amount which would be enough to pay out the car loan
portion in three to eight years, with five being the best goal
(usually). Failing to do this means that you're paying your car
out over 20 years or so—however long the new home loan is—
which means you could still, practically speaking, be paying for
a car years after it's become land-fill.

Warning when buying privately: If you're buying the
vehicle secondhand from a private seller, make sure you get
a written statement from them along the lines of:

'This vehicle (make: model: colour: registration number: and engine number:) is sold free
and clear of all debt by   , on the   day of   200_.

Failure to take these precautions could mean you end up
paying for a car that you can't keep or get your money back on.
See also trick 9, page 115.

CREDIT UNION AUSTRALIA LIMITED
ABN 44 087 650 959
410 Queen Street, Brisbane QLD 4000
GPO Box 100, Brisbane QLD 4001
Phone (07) 3365 0000 Fax (07) 3221 3152

CAR LOAN APPLICATION

All questions/sections of this application must be completed as appropriate. All borrowers must sign the application.

PERSONAL DETAILS

Surname of First Borrower | Given Names | Title

Date of Birth / / | Driver's Licence Number | Membership Number

Residential Address | Postcode

Postal Address (if different) | Postcode

How long have you resided at present address? Years Months | Home Telephone ( )

Previous Residential Address (if less than five years at present address) and period of residence. | Postcode

Period Years Months

Occupation | Employer's Name

Employer's Address | Postcode

Telephone number ( ) | Length of Employment Years Months

Previous Occupation | Previous Employer's Name

Previous Employer's Address | Postcode

Telephone number ( ) | Length of employment Years Months

Surname of Second Borrower | Given Names | Title

Date of Birth / / | Driver's Licence Number | Membership Number

Residential Address | Postcode

Postal Address (if different) | Postcode

How long have you resided at present address? Years Months | Home Telephone ( )

Previous Residential Address (if less than five years at present address) and period of residence. | Postcode

Period Years Months

Occupation | Employer's Name

Employer's Address | Postcode

Telephone number ( ) | Length of Employment Years Months

Previous Occupation | Previous Employer's Name

Previous Employer's Address | Postcode

Telephone number ( ) | Length of Employment Years Months

Are you: ☐ Boarding/Renting   ☐ Buying a house   ☐ Home Owner

Have you ever been bankrupt or insolvent?   YES ☐   NO ☐   (Please attach details)

LOAN PARTICULARS

Amount required this loan: $ | Is this loan to be added to your existing CUA loan? ☐ YES ☐ NO

Proposed repayment per fortnight: $ | or term of loan months

The following motor vehicle details are required.

Is vehicle to be purchased privately? ☐ YES ☐ NO

Make | Model | Year Manufactured | Purchase Price $

Deposit $ | Trade $ | Amount Required $

If known   Registration Number | Chassis Number | Engine Number

Name of any person or company to whom the loan proceeds are to be paid, including any insurers and the amount, if known.

$

$

SAMPLE ONLY

The illustration above is a sample car loan application, to prepare you for the kind of questions you're likely to be asked by most lenders.

Personalised plates: These cost more—anywhere from about $250 to $2000 extra depending on which state you live in—but the revenue is spent on improving road conditions, so you should at least see where your money's going.

Personalised plates trick 1: The cheapest personalised plates are not always advertised on the brochures. Ring the department of transport in your state and ask if they have any other personalised plates on offer at that time. In Queensland recently, for instance, three entire runs of original issue number plates (which had been handed in over the last 50 years or so) were made available for personal issue—using your choice of colours—so you could choose any combination of three letters followed by three numbers, provided they started with either N O or P. (There were some interesting opportunities there, including NUT.001 OOO.001 ONE.234 and ONO.000.) Because they were not worth advertising, they were available for only $275 each, a discount of about $20 off the minimum cost of other personal plates in that state.

Personalised plates trick 2: You can choose from a growing range of colour combinations for your personalised plates, with the idea of choosing one which suits your personality and the colour of your car. But rumour has it that gold writing on red background nearly failed approval in some states because it's difficult to pick up on speed cameras. Not that you need to know that, because you don't speed anyway, now do you?

ALTERNATIVE TO BUYING

Consider renting a small or medium car on bulk rates from a hire company which operates in a major tourist centre (because these are often very cheap). At between $15 and $35 a week—depending on size and popularity—this can be much cheaper than buying. This doesn't work for everyone, but it's certainly worth considering if:

• you live within an hour or two's drive of a major tourist area,
• if your need for a car is likely to fluctuate throughout the year,
• if you're not sure about buying a car,

- or if the idea of ongoing maintenance costs doesn't excite you.

By hiring, instead of buying, you save stacks on repayments, interest rates and annual maintenance and you can swap it for a different colour car nearly as often as you like. (Or if your finances fall on a hard patch, you can swap one rental for a cheaper model at nearly any time, whereas anyone with a car loan is going to have to sit on the rough end of their pine-apple—or refinance, usually at a considerable extra cost!)

The downside is that the car is not yours, so at the end, you have zero resale value. You also miss out on the personal satis-faction of owning your own wheels and the freedom to tinker under the bonnet if you wish—if you don't mind blowing your warranty, that is—or just getting in and driving until the sun sets, without having to worry about penalties for excess kilometres.

11

Slave Seeks Master

You're jobless or in need of a new boss. You've got debts to pay and goals to achieve. It's overwhelming and a little scary. What do you do? How do you start with nothing, and build a comfortable lifestyle not only for yourself, but for your family as well without bludging off everyone who cares about you?

Obviously, you get a(nother) job.

Start by making your own list of employers to investigate and by contacting Centrelink for a list of your local job network providers (free employment agencies).

Did you know?

It's been estimated that Neanderthal man only needed to work about five hours every day to hunt and provide for the family.

After centuries of effort to make our lives easier, we now work an average of three hours every day more than a cave man.

CHOOSE YOUR MASTER

If you want the best chance at actually enjoying the way you earn an income, you should actively choose your career, instead of leaving Chance to tuck it under your pillow. Every year this gets easier and harder at the same time, because your choices are becoming vast.

It helps to be able to identify what skills you have, but if you're new to the workforce, or if you haven't worked for some time or if you're stuck in a job rut that you want to get out of, you can often underestimate yourself. Even basic skills, like gardening, house-cleaning and a 'smiling' telephone voice, can help you earn enough of a living to make yourself comfortably successful.

Try using this talent table to help work out how valuable you really are:

Talent Table

Is this you?	Then you must have:
Can you follow a bus/train/taxi time-table and navigate complicated routes quickly using public transport?	Skills in co-ordinating complicated information.
If the car starts spluttering, do you try to find out what's wrong, working methodically through a list of things it could be and then attempting to fix it?	Problem-solving and mechanical maintenance skills.
Do your friends ask you for help buying cars/furniture/electrical goods/property because you know what to look for and what they're worth?	Technical expertise and possibly negotiating skills.
Do you plan and stick to a budget? Every reader should be able to tick this now! Do you do your own tax return and balance your own bank accounts?	Planning and financial management skills.
Can you divide up household chores and get everyone to pitch in—even your 15-year old daughter who most people can't shift with a bulldozer?	Prioritising, managing, delegation and maybe even negotiation.
Are all your videos labelled and shelved in a particular order. Do you keep diaries for family appointments and calendars to keep track of birthdays and when gardening chores or pet vaccinations are due?	You have various methodical classification skills and can manage information systems.
Can you sew your own clothes choosing machine attachments suitable to each job, or adjust	You have practical, technical and imaginative design skills.

patterns to fit or adjust your relatives' clothes and do you keep your sewing machine maintained, oiling it when required?

Have you ever organised a sausage sizzle, school fete, class party, joint garage sale or sporting event?

You have planning, organisational, teambuilding and delegation skills.

Can you make a limited wardrobe look good for most occasions or tell if something looks right without trying it on?

You have artistic style, presentation and style skills.

Can you present a meal to look as good as the picture on the box or decorate a cake so well that nobody wants to eat it because it looks so good?

You're artistic, creative and you've got excellent visual presentation skills.

Can you design your own diet? Or if you find out someone's coming to your party but they're allergic to some kinds of food, do you research ingredients and recipes to add to or change the menu so they don't have to starve?

You've got information response skills, initiative and scientific investigations skills . . . and you're considerate.

If you have a garden or home-improvement project, can you get quotes from various tradespeople, explaining the project without any trouble and can you imagine what it will look like before it's finished?

You've got research and negotiation abilities, briefing skills and imagination, as well as project planning and budgeting skills.

Do you bet on the races, invest in shares and follow their progress, or run a lotto syndicate? (Not that I advocate betting!)

You've got literacy and numeracy skills. You're also a calculated risk-taker who's methodical and persistent.

Can you keep a group of young children amused by storytelling and various activities? Do the kids enjoy being with you and you with them? Do you pick up other people's kids from school until their parents finish work?

You're creative, (*insane?*) patient and reliable with good communication skills. You've probably got good listening and teaching skills too.

Do you play competitive sports or do you like chess, Monopoly or other games where you get to play with a partner or an opponent?

You're competitive, and may have team skills or leader-ship abilities and be good at planning strategies.

Have you researched your family tree, local history, organisations or government departments?

You're patient, with reading, library, and information systems skills and record-keeping ability.

I could go on and now that you've got the idea, probably you could too. Please do. Sit down with friends or family and make a game of creating a longer list of everything you can do, and then write down how each skill can translate to the work-force—just like this. Then when you see a job vacancy advertised, you just look at the list of skills they want and see which things you've done that you can provide as evidence of your experience.

For example: An ad for a trainee science lab assistant may ask for scientific and research skills, recording and reporting experience and initiative (without specifying tertiary qualifications). So you'd explain that you can accommodate specialist and complex dietary requirements by researching the problem, investigating possibilities and then use your initiative to create and adapt suitable—and still enjoyable—menus. And because you've just finished a 15-generation family tree that spans 17 nations, you have demonstrated research, reporting and recording skills, and you can go on to mention all the other wonderful skills you have which complement it and make it stronger (as shown in the table above).

You don't have to exaggerate or feel like you're fibbing in using these skills when you fill out your job application if you don't have any actual work experience in that particular area. When asked at the interview why you should get the job over someone who has the actual experience in hospitality, for example, you tell the truth:

All my skills and experience relate directly to the ones needed for the job. I may not have received payment for organising family functions, but I not only managed it, I enjoyed it thoroughly. My last function was reported in the local newspaper as being one of the best attended and largest reunions the district had ever seen. I've also been on call with local nursing homes for organising outings and celebrations involving food, entertainment, venues and special treats to make the moment memorable for everyone.

Heck, they should hire you on the spot.

Remember: it's energy and excitement that employers are

attracted to. They can 'feel' it through your words, so let your personality show. Your personality can be marketable for them—it translates almost directly to profits.

Be yourself, because nobody else can be.

MIXING WORK WITH SCHOOL

If it's your first job you're looking for, you can now combine school studies with work placement and job training, and earn yourself points towards an industry qualification AND finish your Year 12 certificate at the same time. To make things easier, you can split your week between school days and work days (and get paid while you're at work).

JOB TRAINING AT SCHOOL

If you're in Years 9 or 10, this is your chance to learn about different careers and get some of the skills employers are hunting for—long before you leave school. If you're in Years 11 or 12 now, you can try getting on-the-job training in an industry which interests you (ie. technology, tourism, biotechnology etc).

NEW APPRENTICESHIPS

If you're having trouble staying motivated at school AND if you're in Year 11 or 12, consider going for a 'New apprenticeship'. That's where you can earn a wage while you're at work—even if it's through the day, when you'd normally be at school. For more information ring the Centrelink Hotline, 1800 639 629.

Defence force cadets should soon be accredited within the framework for national training too, so stay tuned for greater opportunities to develop self-esteem, leadership skills and a greater understanding of the community.

PREPARATION FOR THE JOB APPLICATION OR INTERVIEW

No matter whether it's your first or your fifth job you're going for, you need to prepare for the interview. Having been on both sides of the interviewer's desk and having processed literally thousands of job applications over almost a decade, I know some of the pitfalls and tricks that will help separate you from the pack.

Trick 1: Before phoning, check out the company's website, product brochures, and if it's a company that's listed on the stock exchange even try checking out their annual report for any inside information. (Annual reports for listed companies are free upon request. You just have to ring their shareholder relations officer at head office, and ask them to post one to you. To tell if a company is listed, just check out the financial reports in your biggest local paper or in the *Australian Financial Review.* Some of them are abbreviated, but they're all there, listed alphabetically.) Yes, it is a bit more effort and if you do this for every job application, you may go completely nuts. But it's a great way to find out about employers you're really interested in, their capacity to pay you and prospects for promotion. It also arms you with vital information you can use in your application or interview. To walk into an interview with their annual report under your arm looks impressive. It demonstrates your initiative, planning and thoroughness.

Trick 2: When asking about the job at the application stage, also take the opportunity to ask about many of the things you'll be itching to know about if you get the job, but can't ask during the interview without running the risk of giving the employer the wrong impression about you. Things like:

- **Salary scale**—starting rate, and what the top rate is after how many years.
- **Probationary periods**—is the first six or 12 months only a trial period before they assess you to see if they wish to make you permanent?
- **Paydays**—if they're weekly, fortnightly or monthly.

- **Holidays**—how many weeks are there a year and do you have to take them all at once or can you split them so you can take shorter breaks more regularly through the year? Also ask about leave-loading (also called holiday bonuses): if you're entitled to any, and if so, at what rate?
- **If you're in the defence forces or emergency services reserves**—you'll also need to know if that particular employer is prepared to cope with unexpected periods of absence, ensuring that they are aware of government incentive schemes to help them cope while you're away.
- **If you're female with a not-so-obvious bun in the oven**—you might want to know what your entitlements to maternity leave are before you apply for the job. You're not obliged to inform any employer that you're pregnant, because they're not permitted by law to discriminate against you, but failing to tell them during your interview could be considered deceitful, making workplace relations uncomfortable to say the least, whereas honesty could go either way towards landing you the job. I have seen heavily pregnant women win permanent jobs on at least seven occasions within a few months. On most occasions, the employers happily agreed to hold off starting dates until after the births of the babies—such is the great desire in some workplaces for keen and honest staff!
- **Overtime and travel**—Some jobs put limitations on how far away from home you can travel on your days off, if you're on call. (*On call* means they can call you at home any time of the day or night and ask you to be at work within a few minutes.) Some jobs practically own your every waking hour through overtime, double shifts and interstate travel and make you feel obliged to work, whether it's Christmas Eve or not. So asking if overtime is expected—or if it's voluntary as required—*before* your interview could rescue you from the embarrassing situation of your jaw dropping on the floor when you find out just how much of your 'free' time you're expected to give freely to the company.

- **Staff discounts and health benefits for staff**—ask if they offer any.
- **Public transport**—ask what, if any, public transport is convenient to the workplace. For example, a train station or bus stop within easy walking distance could help you put off buying a car until you can pay cash for most of it.
- **Union membership**—ask if it's compulsory (and check out the next chapter Understanding your Paypacket for more information).
- **Superannuation**—ask if it's compulsory with this employer for you to contribute to super IN ADDITION to the legislated 9% that your employer pays on your behalf. If so, ask what the percentage is that's currently required (often between 3% and 5%), if it's employer-sponsored, meaning that your employer puts in money too (in proportion to your contributions and on top of the required 9%). Or ask if you can nominate your own super fund. (See Understanding your Paypacket for more information.)

No, you're not going to choose your job based on any one of these points in particular. To do that—particularly if you're unemployed—would be nothing short of foolish. The idea is to prepare yourself as much as possible for the interview. This knowledge—if you can get it—gives you confidence. It also prevents you from having to ask these questions during the interview, which may leave them thinking that you're only interested in what you can get out of the company.

For example, it's much better to ask for confirmation: 'I understand the salary scale starts at $28,000 and rises to $38,000 over seven years?' than it is to say, 'How much ya gunna pay me?'

It also gives you something to contribute to the conversation, helping to make it a two-way street, rather than making you feel like you're a target being bombed with questions for the entire time.

It's worth asking some of these questions over the phone,

even though the person taking your call might not know the answer. It helps you raise questions more intelligently during the interview—eg. 'The gentleman who took my call when I originally applied wasn't able to tell me if I had to be in a union. Is there any requirement?'

Just be careful not to make their existing staff out to be idiots—even if they are. Remember, someone had to have hired them too at some stage. Chances are it could be the people you are talking to now—or worse, one of your interviewers could be related to them. Besides, if there is a problem with their phone staff it's a good bet your interviewers know about the problem already, so they'll get the message without you having to make it obvious.

Trick 3: Before leaving, ask if you can be considered for temporary or casual work if you're unsuccessful—just in case. Surprisingly often, applicants who win the job have already been appointed to another job in the meantime, leaving the interviewers to look up the next best applicant on their list. Very often, they'd much rather keep lists of people they've interviewed for a few months and call you up again later if another vacancy pops up, than go through the whole expensive and time-consuming processes of re-advertising, re-shortlisting and re-interviewing. You would too, if you were busy.

EMPLOYMENT SERVICES

There are two main kinds of employment services: job network providers and recruitment agencies.

Job network providers are private companies which are government subsidised and linked to Centrelink. You have to be registered with at least one provider soon after applying for Youth Allowance or Job Search (Newstart) Allowance. Centrelink can give a free list of job providers in your area, or see the *Yellow Pages* under 'employment agencies'.

Job network providers replace the old Commonwealth Employment Service (CES) by acting as the cupid between employers and job seekers. Employers notify them of vacancies and skills required; job seekers provide them with details of skills and availability, and they attempt to find the perfect matches by sending along a small selection of applicants for the employer to choose from.

Job network providers also provide free facilities and free services to help you find a job, including typing up résumés, use of computers, internet access to check out jobsearch websites and photocopying and fax facilities. If you're registered with them, their services should all be free.

You have to register with the job network provider in order to be considered for their vacancy lists, otherwise they don't get paid by the government for helping you find a job. Each job network provider has two vacancy lists: a) the list that's 'linked' to Centrelink and which is available to all job providers on the network, and b) the jobs that are phoned through to that particular job provider directly by any local employers.

Handy hint: To save time looking up the different job vacancy lists, register with up to five job network providers at a time—provided you're only registered with ONE for advance-level assistance. (Advance assistance is where a case manager is assigned to you for one-on-one intensive help to get you trained —if necessary—and get you that job.)

Once you get the job, the employer pays you directly and you can finish up with the job network provider.

Recruitment agencies sub-contract your services to employers who need short- or medium-term replacements. Most agencies specialise in the kind of employee they offer to provide. Some cater for trade apprentices or unskilled trainees, while others may specialise in information technology, medical staff or office personnel—see your local *Yellow Pages* for a list of companies close to you.

Agencies differ from job network providers in that you will have to pass a test or assessment before you can register. That's so they can determine your skill levels and guarantee them to employers in order to negotiate the best fee. Employers pay the agency and the agency pays you. So even after you get the job, you're not finished with the employment agency. If they can't find you any work, they can sometimes apply for 'stand down' for you from the government so you can get Centrelink payments without a long waiting period.

Warning: 'Stand downs' require evidence that no jobs are available for you and that every avenue to find you a job has been explored—and this can be hard to provide.

Hint: Before registering, ask how often the agency has had to do this in the past, or if they pay you a small wage from a contingency fund until they can find you work again. (Contingency funds are rare at the time of writing, but rumoured to be coming soon on a wider scale.)

ADDITIONAL WARNINGS

1. If an employment agency or job network provider asks you to pay for anything—for example, a photographic shoot to put together a portfolio if you want to be a model or actor—then be suspicious, be *veeery* suspicious. Ask if you can shop around to get the work done elsewhere to use for the résumé—and if they refuse to accept this, then there's a fair chance they make more money out of getting clients to pay these fees than they do in earning commissions by finding people worthwhile jobs.

2. Newspaper ads posted on telephone poles and in supermarkets offering $1000 a week working from home are usually suck-ins to get you to buy business kits, again under the principle of making more money out of milking you dry selling the kits than selling good product to clients.

12

Understanding your Paypacket

This chapter is about the things you need to know about your paypacket once you do land that job, from superannuation, payroll deductions and union memberships to tax obligations, payment methods and allowances. It includes as many little tricks, traps and hints that I could think of to help you get the best out of every cent you earn.

Naturally, every paypacket is different. Every employer has their own arrangements on payment; some even have the ability to pay electronically but refuse to use all the possible features, because it's 'too much trouble'. Such employers really annoy me actually, because I've worked in pay offices for over a decade and I know exactly how 'much trouble' it ISN'T to use many of the options available for electronic transfers of funds.

But we can't *make* employers do anything more than credit our salaries or wages to our accounts. They each set up rules based on what they're prepared to do and it's these rules which we have to learn to work inside (or around). For example:

If you work for a SMALL employer who pays by cheque consider opening an account with the same bank they do business banking with every day, and ask the person who does the banking (who usually works closely with the person who does the pays) to bend the rules for you by transferring the funds directly into your account.

It's better for you, because you don't have to wait until you get a chance to bank your cheque or wait for clearances. And it's better for them, because there's no cheque fees or government tax for writing the cheque.

If you work for ANY employer who insists on paying by cash, make sure you get an official payslip. Particularly since the introduction of GST, payment by cash may be an indication that your employer is being naughty with their tax obligations. If you don't keep payslips with details of what tax they claim to have deducted for you, you might end up having to pay tax again.

Payslips and group certificates are your proof that your employer advised you that tax was deducted properly. Keep them safe!

Penalties for tax evasion can have so many zeros, you need two hands to count them. Failure to report tax evasion can be nasty too. So make sure you get your payslips with their company logo or signature on them.

Definition Alert!

Group certificates are the mother of all payslips, detailing everything you got paid by that employer for the year. They can look like a letter or like your payslip—except you usually get two copies: one to keep and one to forward with your tax return. Your employer also gets two copies: one to send to the ATO within 14 days and one to keep.

If you work for an employer who transfers money electronically into your personal account, ask if they are able or willing to split your pay and send part of it to one account and part of it to another. Some employers have few or no limits on how many different directions your pay can be sent; but all will request that you nominate one account—your grocery savings account or mortgage offset account perhaps—as a default in which you want partial pays or any surplus monies to be deposited.

Example: Getting your employer to split your pay to send $50 to your child's university account at ABC credit union; $45 to your Christmas account at XYZ bank; $6 to DEF insurance to pay for your contents insurance; and $220 to GHI building society for your car loan, while the rest goes into your mortgage offset account at JKL bank is like switching a good portion of your budgeting and bill paying over to automatic, so you don't have to worry about it.

I'm NOT recommending you let your bank accounts get complicated. Usually splitting your financial eggs between two financial institutions is sufficient, because you can set up transfer authorities to split up your pay amongst other accounts. But it's also very handy having more than one bank to go to if you need cash in a hurry when their computers are on the blink—especially if you live in smaller towns or regional Australia.

DEDUCTIONS

Ask your employer about all the different kinds of automatic deductions they can arrange from your pay. Possibilities include: memberships and contributions to ambulance and health funds, car and house insurance companies, collection agencies, life insurance, private superannuation, extra tax (explained soon), and child support agencies—to name a few. So ask your payroll officer if they can show you what's available.

SECURITY

Payslips should be made available promptly and all details on them are confidential. While a rough idea of how much you earn may be known or guessed at, your employer has a responsibility to ensure that other employees are not aware of your specific financial circumstances, no matter where on the corporate structure you are employed. Payslips should therefore be sealed in a way that doesn't allow any figures to be read by holding the payslip to the light. They should also be sealed in a way that ensures you can tell if they've been opened without your authority (your paymaster excluded).

PERSONAL INCOME TAX AND PRECAUTIONS

Tax scales are tables supplied by the Australian Tax Office so your pay office can tell how much tax they have to extract from your paypacket. Unless you have a rental property, the closest you get to this money is the smell of the ink on your payslip. I suggest you get yourself a copy of the scales to share with your workmates, as this is the only way to make sure your employer is deducting the right amount of tax for you—before you get a ferocious tax bill at the end of the year. *Note:* Copies are available free from newsagents. Scales for weekly pays are usually on white paper, while scales for fortnightly pays are usually yellow.

It's the ATO's job to suck as much tax as it can from your wallet and it's your job to claim as much of it back as you can (legally of course). The best way to do that if you're one of the millions who doesn't have an accountant is to READ your next Tax Pack instead of turning it into worm food. It will open your eyes to deductions and rebates that you might not realise previously existed. (For example, donations to the Australian film industry have a different value to donations to other areas of the arts.)

Did you know?

You have 28 days after starting work to provide your tax file number to your employer or your tax will go up to 48.5%. Protect yourself by getting a tax declaration form (from any post office or from your employer) **because you won't get the extra back until you send in your tax return. Ouch!**

HINT FOR TAX REBATES YOU CAN CLAIM

Many people like to claim rebates at the end of the financial year so they get a nice fat tax refund to splurge mid-year or in time for Christmas. But you can get the best out of these rebates by claiming them through your paypacket every pay and automatically increasing your mortgage or car loan repayments accordingly so you can't spend the extra money by accident. If you're entitled to the top dependent spouse rebate, doing this will cut up to *seven years* off your $100,000 25-year mortgage at current interest rates!

You can claim a rebate:

- if you have a dependent spouse with no dependent children: this will be either a $1324 per annual refund or up to $50.30 less taken out of your pay each fortnight.
- if you are a sole parent: up to $1243 per year or up to $47.20 per fortnight
- if you have a dependent parent or parent-in-law: up to $1190 per year or up to $45.20 per fortnight (See? It can be good having your parents around!)
- if you have a dependent relative who is an invalid: $596 per year = $22.60 per fortnight.

There are also zone rebates available, depending on which remote or regional area you live and work in. And there's the savings rebate, if you're an eligible pensioner or a self-funded retiree who's still working to some extent.

SUPERANNUATION: GENERAL

Known affectionately as 'super', this is a *super* way of saving for your retirement. There are generous tax concessions for contributions—see Tax Pack or your accountant for the latest rates—and it's a way of ensuring that you're building at least some wealth throughout your working life to help pay for Tim Tams and other essentials when you're old enough to give your boss the carrot.

There is, however, a LOT of suspicion about superannuation, mainly because of the faceless nature of the big superannuation funds, the number of smaller superannuation funds that go bust leaving their members high and dry, the growing compulsory percentage that's being paid into super in lieu of payrises, the length of time over which you have to have 'faith' that it's being invested wisely, and the incredible number of changes in governing legislation that have occurred over the last few years under various governments.

To some extent, you're still placing bets on what the conditions and values of your payout will eventually be. Sadly, some funds still encourage suspicion by forecasting payouts with returns which are actually much higher than what they've actually been achieving. In 2000 for example, one major superannuation fund suffered a *negative* return of nearly 5% after boasting of returns closer to 14%—and that's before you consider their ferocious annual fees!

> **Beware of superannuation funds which promise returns that are higher than the going rates for half-yearly term deposits unless they're prepared to put their money where their mouths are by supplying a capital guarantee of some kind.**

COMPULSORY FOR WHO?

Superannuation is usually only compulsory for the *employee* themselves to pay into for permanent employees—either full or part-time—in a state or other government department or other corporation which chooses to do so. Government legislation DOES, however, make it compulsory for ALL *employers* to pay into a superannuation fund on behalf of each employee, (from 1 July at a rate of 9%) of your annual base rate salary.

Where employers DO insist that their employees also contribute to the superannuation fund, compulsory rates for the employee are usually between 3% and 5% of your base fortnightly salary rate (excluding late shifts and other payments). Five percent is the standard; however you can apply for the lower rates if you apply for an exemption on the basis of hardship (for example).

EMPLOYER-SPONSORED

Employers—particularly government departments—may also participate in employer-sponsored superannuation schemes. This is where your employer not only pays the minimum super required by law, but also contributes a certain amount for every dollar that you contribute. Government departments currently contribute a total of 12.75% of your annual salary if you work for them. That's about $2.55 for every dollar you pay in!

Obviously, if your employer participates in an employer-sponsored scheme like this, you would have to be close to insane not to contribute the maximum allowable percentage of your wage each pay if you can afford it. It's practically free money.

SALARY SACRIFICE (VOLUNTARY CONTRIBUTIONS FROM YOUR PAY)

There are generous tax concessions for making voluntary contributions into a superannuation fund which is not sponsored by your employer, or for voluntary contributions over and above the amount that your employer is prepared to match (in its chosen proportion and in addition to the required 9%.) But this money is effectively locked away until you retire.

If you're young, it pays to do your sums. Even with generous tax concessions, you may be better off devoting some or all of your spare cash to extra car or mortgage repayments, instead of voluntary or extra superannuation contributions—especially if you've still got 15 years or more until you retire.

You may choose to go with the fund that your employer chooses to use because of the industry they're in. Employers of mechanics, for instance, may have to go with the superannuation fund made available through the motor trades association. If your employer has made it compulsory for you to pay into their fund on top of their compulsory contribution, then the only way you can change things is to convince your employer that they can do better for all of its staff elsewhere. Remember, their retirement savings are at stake too, so convincing them may not be as difficult as you think.

UNION MEMBERSHIP
Depending on government policy at the time, membership in a union is either compulsory or voluntary. If it's compulsory, the only way you can get out of paying membership fees is by donating the same amount of money as your membership fee to charity and presenting the receipt to your employer and to the union secretary as evidence. But even then, you can have trouble getting or keeping your job if the other staff are all in the one union and gang up on you. (And arguably you are bludging on any union-achieved improvements in conditions if you haven't contributed.)

The employer will certainly know if their staff are militant on the subject of union membership, so ask what the union obligations are towards the end of your job interview. Some unions are particularly expensive, some are compulsory even for casual or part-time staff, and sometimes automatic deductions from every pay are encouraged instead of lump sum payments.

So if you have a choice of unions to join—as is often the case for many jobs in the public service—compare these points as well as the union's track record before choosing which union to join.

HOT TIPS FOR TAX TIME (USING PAYPACKET TRICKS)

1. Annual tax bills can be a fairly common problem for people who work lots of shifts or overtime—you can do one of two things to avoid the problem:

   a) be happy and put the amount you've calculated you'll have to pay in your mortgage offset account or credit card to keep interest down until it's time to cough up to the Tax Office, or

   b) ask your employer to increase the tax that's taken out of your paypacket by a set amount every pay. Twenty dollars is a fairly common choice, although you can work it out more closely if you've been getting roughly the same bill for a few years in a row.

Did you know?

One large employer I'm aware of employs about 8000 shift workers, and at one stage about 40% of them voluntarily elected to pay extra tax to avoid getting tax bills.

One of those employees has rather sneakily chosen to pay an extra $240 every fortnight, just so his wife couldn't spend it. He blows his humungous tax refund every year on treats for himself, telling her he had a win at work with lotto. One day soon, I'm sure she'll wonder why he always wins lotto in August.

---

2. Keeping your payslips clipped together—under a bulldog clip or in a ringbound folder—will help you at tax time. Use them to count up all the meal allowances you were paid in addition to your overtime (m/a's are not taxable) and make sure they've been listed separately on your group certificate. If they're not listed separately, then they may have been lumped in with your total earnings. Compare the year-to-date gross total on your last payslip with your group certificate to see if the meal allowances make a difference and answer Question 2 on your tax return with the information you discover by doing this.

3. Also use your file of payslips to make sure your superannuation contributions were increased at least once during the year. If you had a payrise, they're supposed to be increased in proportion to any basic payrises you've received in the last 12 months. If this doesn't happen then you'll miss out on some serious pension entitlements by the time you retire.

Handy hint on the subject of super contributions: If your payrise was due to a promotion, you can ask your super fund—if it allows this—to accept a back payment from you so that the super contribution goes up at the same time your pay did—it should actually be done at the same time anyway. But if it's been missed AND if you choose to backpay to your promotion date AND if your super fund is employer-sponsored (meaning your employer puts in two to four dollars for every dollar you put in) THEN your employer will have to stick in their proportionate backpay too. Yippeee for you.

4. Use your file of payslips to keep track of any EXTRA superannuation contributions you make on top of the standard contributions and use the total to claim a rebate at R4 on your tax return. Your super fund should also send you a statement confirming this amount.

5. Paying additional superannuation contributions on behalf of your spouse is very convenient when your employer lets you do it straight from your paypacket. See Tax Pack or your accountant for explanations of the great tax incentives attached to doing this. If you're still young, it won't interest you so much, because your money will be locked up for ages. But if you're within ten years of retirement it's one of the best investment options you have.

Handy hint: If your payroll system doesn't allow extra super deductions for your spouse, try sticking them into your mortgage offset account or overdraft—or even your credit card—to reduce your interest all year, and then pay it as a lump sum in the last week of the financial year so you still get the rebate in time. If you let it sit in your credit card, you can draw it out as a cash advance—remembering that it's okay to let your credit card get overpaid, especially if it pays you interest when it is.

13

How NOT to Get Suckered by Salespeople

Okay, so you've got the best deal on your house and car, and your job's sorted out. What about the times when you need to fork out some of that hard-earned cash for life's essentials? Like everything else we've covered, there are smart and not so smart ways to do it. When I first started out, I often fell victim to all sorts of sales tricks. That's how I came to learn all the nasty little games that I'm about to show you so you don't have to experience them for youself.

The door-to-door sales pests and phone marketers are classic examples.

DOOR-TO-DOOR SALESPEOPLE AND PHONE MARKETERS
Their advantages:
- *Surprise!* By catching you off-guard, they can slip in a few good lines to appeal to your pride, jealousy or desires before you can mentally prepare yourself for a sales pitch.
- *Research!* Phone marketers often buy lists of client details from large corporate companies, which sometimes give them an insight into your personal interests—still obeying strict privacy laws. For example, from an insurance company they might only get your phone number—without your

name, which makes it legal under privacy legislation. But having asked for a list of swimming pool owners, or vintage car drivers or whatever in the first place, they have a fair idea of how to target your interests quickly.

Door-to-door salespeople do their research in person. As they approach your house, they prepare themselves— checking out your standard of living, any obvious hobbies or interests, what kind of neighbours you have, your gardens, if any. Even the colours you choose for your house can tell them something about you, even before they see your face. So when you open the door, they already have a fair idea of what they are going to say to arouse your interest and keep your attention long enough to make their sale.

- *Rehearsal!* Before they set foot in your street, door-to-door salespeople have rehearsed practically every kind of approach there is for their product, and will have an intriguing range of responses ready for nearly every kind of refusal that you could politely—or otherwise—throw back at them. No matter what you say, it's their job to say something that will make you realise that there is something missing in your life—something that they can provide for you—at a special price and for a limited time only! And they practise, and practise and practise, before they come for you.
- *Mindset!* Their game is one of percentages. They know they won't get sales at every door—or with every call—so they just keep trying, practising different approaches, learning each time, and getting better. And with each door closed— or with every phone slammed—they know they're getting one step closer to a sale. After all, they present a reasonable product with a convincing sales pitch, and the price is right—yet still, for a limited time only. If you feel guilty—as I used to—for turning them away, just remember, by buying their product and helping them to make a living out of bullying—politely or otherwise—people into buying things that they don't really want or need, you're not doing them any favours.

Tips for turning off telemarketers and door-to-door salespeople:
You could just say 'no thanks' and hang up or close the door, but these are a bit more fun:

1. When they ask, 'How are you today?' tell them about your runny nose, your dead cat and your flat tyre—who else would listen?
2. If they want to loan you money, tell them you just filed for bankruptcy so you could sure use some money.
3. Tell them you're on home detention and that you'll talk it over if they bring you a case of beer, chips and a crate of cartridges for your shotgun.
4. Tell them you can't give your credit card details over the phone or to door-to-door people because you cancelled it after the last telemarketer salesperson ripped you off.

And a little more seriously:

5. If they say they're Flo Schmo from ABC Incorporated, ask them to spell their name, their company name, its location, phone numbers etc. Then tell them you'll have to get back in contact with them later because you have to check them out with Consumer Affairs to make sure they're not a mob of crooks first.
6. Tell them you can't talk now and can they ring you or call back in a fortnight, and in the meantime can they send you an information pack so you can check out if their product is crappy or not. Tell them if they're not prepared to send you an information pack, then don't bother calling back.
7. If there's a time limit before the offer runs out, tell them you'll have to miss the opportunity this time round, because you don't get pressured into anything and certainly not over a few hundred bucks in savings or less.

Always remember, your contact details are supposed to be confidential. If a telemarketer has them, you have a right to know how they got them—particularly if you have a silent number, in which case you may have grounds to file a complaint or to request an investigation both with the tele-marketing company and with your phone service provider.

THE YES MAN

Yes men are highly trained salespeople who ask you very short (not always polite) questions that are specifically designed for a 'yes' response: Would you like to win a new car? Do you want the best for your children's futures? Would you like me to show you how to turn $10 into $1000 without risk?

'No idiot, I like driving my old bomb; I want my kids to bludge off me for life; and I want to stay poor forever.'

Of course you're hardly likely to answer 'no' to any one of these. And that's their intent. The problem is, that even if you don't actually say the word 'yes' aloud, just thinking it can get them inside your head.

Your defence: Well, you could be rude and slam the door, turn your back and walk off, or hurl abuse at them until they go away, but there's enough grief in the world now—we don't need any more. Besides, this response will only rob you of an opportunity to be gracious, and will probably leave you a little grumpier for a while afterwards too.

So you might try:

- 'No thank you. It's my policy not to buy anything that's sold by telemarketers door-to-door,' and then politely but deter-minedly close your door. OR . . .
- 'No thank you, I don't have time to talk right now, but if you get me an information pack I'll read it and get back to you if I'm interested.' (*Would you like to give me your phone number so that I can call you and save you the hassle?* they'll ask. No, thank you. I'll call you, you say.)

DO NOT: Allow them to drag out the conversation.

AND NEVER give them your name, home phone number, credit card numbers or an invitation to come back later.

TRY NOT to use the 'Yeah sure, but …' response, because you're only giving them an opening to defend themselves. And the last thing you want is to spend your Sunday afternoon arguing on your doorstep or over the phone with a salesperson.

REMEMBER: Clever budgeting means planning major purchases ahead of time: shopping around for quality and prices, comparing brands, warranties, colours, attachments, special features and flashing lights. It *doesn't mean* being cornered into parting with big bucks (for something you only partially want) during your favourite TV show.

Did you know?

I once had the rather entertaining experience of being approached by an L-plate con-artist. Being a rather observant little hawk myself, I had noticed him working his way up the street while I was gardening. But feeling rather cheeky that day, I let him play his little game while I counted how many mistakes he made.

- He omitted to hide the fact that after each house, he would stop for about ten minutes to fill out a little notebook. I saw him do it. *But why*, I wondered, would he do that?
- After invading my quiet afternoon, he pressed me for my name—he couldn't have discovered it otherwise, since I was new to the neighbourhood and I had a silent phone number. But when I gave him Jezie Belle as an obvious nickname, he let his irritation show.
- He mistook my interest as genuine at one stage, so he couldn't refuse my request to look through the receipt book for myself without appearing to be hiding something.
- And yes, his receipt book turned out to be the mysterious little notebook that I'd seen him filling in earlier. After finding out each of my neighbours' names, the industrious fellow had taken the time to forge receipts for the same handful of neighbours, four or five times over throughout his book. Sure, it made his sales book look impressive. It also made it easier for him to flick

through to find my neighbours' names to point them
out to me. But it was also painfully apparent that my
neighbour with a brick house across the road would
hardly buy aluminium cladding—four times.

PUSHY SALESPEOPLE

They treat you like a mug, don't they?

'I've got to have your decision now, lady. That price is only
good for one day.'

Give me a break!

Sadly, there's not much we can do about them other than
turn our backs and walk away, or ask if there's another salesperson available—with a grin on your face. Try asking for
prices 'for comparison', telling them that you have to roll
investments out before you can buy, so you need to be told
prices that are good for a fortnight.

Car and computer salespeople are notorious for telling you
they have to check their prices with the manager before they
can give you even the foggiest idea on price—and then they
leave you sitting in their office for ages scratching your backside
or picking your nose.

Don't put up with this. Your time is valuable too. If they
don't look like returning quickly, leave their office and walk
around the showroom, or outside the building for fresh air. It
makes them nervous that you'll leave, especially if you're
eyeing off the showroom with their competition across the
street. Check out their landscaping ideas if nothing else, but
never discuss anything about the sale or your current finances
in an empty office, because some unscrupulous firms make sure
the manager or salesperson in the next office can hear every
word you say.

If they leave you unattended for too long, use their note-
paper to leave either a note with your phone number for them
to call you when they're ready, or a note to say you'll call them
after you've compared prices and service elsewhere.

SUSPICIOUS SUCK-INS

Pick up almost any daily newspaper and you should be able to find at least one suspicious advertisement—usually in the classifieds section under 'business opportunities'. But occasionally, you'll see the bolder cons advertised in more brazen ads like the one below.

This ad was lifted from a reputable newspaper a few months ago. Only the phone number and town have been changed. Everything else is word for word. The ad measured an eye-catching 15cm x 7cm, which was a little over half a page wide and two column inches long.

LOCAL INVESTORS WANTED

We have more business than we can handle in the Woopwoop area and are offering local investors the opportunity to share in our success.

If you have $20,000 or more available and would be interested in getting a 25% return on your money, without taking unnecessary risks, we would like to talk to you.

Phone the owner on 0400 000 000 for details of this exciting offer.

WARNING BELLS FROM THE AD

This ad is the perfect example of a classic potential con with all the signs that should set warning bells clanging in your ears.

1. The contact phone number is a mobile number only.
2. There's no contact name—not even a first name.
3. The company's name, ABN, ACN and other contact details are missing, and the 25% return on investment is a tad on the generous side for a company that's not prepared to publish who they are.

4. $20,000 is a little on the large size for a minimum invest-
   ment. Your average prospectus issued by most companies
   offers an entry minimum around $2000 to $10,000, with
   $2000 being the more common entry value by far.
5. Legitimate companies that need to raise money don't have
   to advertise so haphazardly. They can do it faster, easier
   and sometimes cheaper through a reputable enterprise
   market. See also page 155.
6. They also made the mistake of boasting about having 'too
   much business' in a large regional town in which existing
   businesses have struggled for years and new businesses are
   not embraced quickly by the community. (Even some major
   chainstores have problems!)

Warning bells from ringing the number
It's always wisest to proceed with caution when attempting to
ring numbers like these, because unless you have your caller-ID
blocked, today's technology makes it practically child's play to
record your incoming phone number and trace records to
discover your name, address and anything else in which a
professional con-person might have an interest.

So to avoid having your private information tracked or
misused, try calling from a phone booth, from a workplace
where outgoing calls go through a company switchboard—
paying your boss for the private call of course!—or from a
silent home phone number which has your caller-ID blocked.
(Ring your phone provider for more details.)

Things that were wrong with this particular phone call
included:
1. The mobile was answered by a recording that politely
   advised me '. . . not to waste your time or cost of the phone
   call, leave your name and contact details after the tone'. But
   let's face it, if I was interested in investing $20,000 for 25%
   return, then a $1 tax deductible phone call is hardly likely
   to bother me. Obviously, what's going on here is the door-
   to-door salesperson scenario where you still have to open

the door (this time it's by you ringing them). And you still get greeted by someone who chooses the time and place to hit you with their spiel . . . making sure that *you* are the one that's caught off-guard, and not them.

2. Still no contact names provided, although it was a man's voice on the recording. Phone recordings for investment cons usually do seem to have a man's voice on them, by the way. Perhaps they think a man's voice sounds more like 'money' talking? I was half expecting a female voice, however, as quite a few nasty schemes use legitimate telephone answering services as 'fronts' for their own little networks. That way they can do without the expense of a formal business address *and* have a nice sounding 'secretary' to answer their phones up to 24 hours a day—while they still get the benefit of your contact details so they can ring you at a time of their convenience. So always ask the person who answers the phone if they are an answering service or an employee of the company.

3. At least I learned the company name this time, but it didn't make me feel very much better. As suspected, it was a 'national' company—which, if you want to be cynical, just means they are able to con people all over the country. Sadly, I can't mention the company's name here, because after researching them further for this chapter, I discovered they're already involved in legal action—and I don't want to get mixed up in that mess at all.

However, I can say that their company name gave away enough about them; anyone with an eighth-grade education could guess they were a last-chance 'finance' company for seriously in-debt people who want to get even deeper in debt by buying certain thingies—in this case, computers.

And what was it they said about taking unnecessary risks? I'd like to know their definition of *risky*!

Note: Some legitimate companies operating in smaller towns or country areas may feel compelled from time to time to advertise anonymously like this to try to keep their competitors

---

Did you know?
For a fee, anyone can check out a company's legitimacy through the Australian Securities and Investment Commission, phone 1300 300 630 or website: www.asic.com.au

---

from learning what they're up to. But in reality, in small towns and country areas, you don't keep secrets for long anyway. And as a business—in Australia particularly, where we all love to support our Aussie battlers—you're more likely to rally support from the community if you're open about your problems or expansion plans from the beginning. So advertising like this may in the long run hurt you more than you expect. And in the short term you could be classified as a potential con and ignored. So if you're legitimate and operating in Australia, then you shouldn't be ashamed to publish your company's name, office street address (not a PO box), contact phone number (not only a mobile or answering service) and a trusted employee's contact name. Or as previously mentioned, try listing on a reputable enterprise market as detailed below.

Definition Alert!
The enterprise market is intended to be a means of raising capital for companies who are too small or do not wish to be listed on the stock exchange. Also known as a Business Equity Matching Service, these opportunity markets operate much like a dating service by matching investors with opportunities in small, medium-sized and emerging growth businesses according to your investment goals. Fee structures vary so ask before you try.

For example Westpak Business Equity Matching Service – 1300 363 831 or website www.westpac. com.au – charges the company not the investor, usually about $110 for six months plus a 4% success fee up to

---

$2,000,000 raised with a minimum of $4000 and 2% thereafter. Some focus on rural and regional opportunities, like the Bendigo Stock Exchange – Ph: (03) 5444 0055 or website www.bsx.com.au/home.asp. Note: As with all investments, investigate thoroughly yourself.

BE SUSPICIOUS

The only way to avoid sales snares is to stay on the lookout for cons as much as possible. Be suspicious. Be *veeerry* suspicious.

About the only time you can relax a bit is when you're shopping in major national chainstores which carry enough market weight to influence the quality of product that's supplied by their contractors. Their parent companies are nearly all listed on the stock exchange, which means they also have to meet strict compliance rules. They also understand what loss of customer faith can do to their share price as well as their profits. So major chain stores will always refund or replace purchases you're not happy with, and in terms of sales strategies, they are pretty much limited to subliminal techniques which are a lot less stressful to deal with.

So, dealing with reputable companies is a shortcut to dodging most of the horrid little shopping landmines, those great deals that always blow up in your face.

Even if you're careful, there are still likely to be one or two occasions when you're landed with a lemon, short-changed or left feeling like a sucker. When that happens, adjust your attitude. Take control, learn your lesson, and seek legal restitution if possible.

For consumer protection relating to:
• Warranties, refunds, defective or dangerous products, and resolution of individual consumer problems—ring the Office of Fair Trading in your state (sometimes known as Consumer Affairs). Contact numbers are:

NSW: 13 32 20   Vic: 03 9627 6000   Tas: 1300 654 499
Qld: 07 3246 1500   WA: 1300 304 054   SA: 08 8204 9777
NT: 08 8999 5184
  Or for:
- GST or price exploitation, unconscionable or anti-competitive conduct, restrictive trading, collusive tendering or resolution of your personal consumer problem which affects many other people or an industry—ring the Australian Competition and Consumer Commission on 1800 802 715.

  But if they can't help you and if you have no idea who else to ring, then try Countrylink, a free Commonwealth government advisory service on 1800 026 222 for a referral. They won't be able to help you, but they can give you a list of people who can. *Note:* Countrylink is targeted as a service for people living outside metropolitan areas.

14

Smart Shopping: Save Money while you Spend

SAVING MONEY BY COST CUTTING

Remember: Budgeting and shopping must be fun, fast and easy. You shouldn't feel like you have to drag yourself around to every shop in town hunting down savings of a few dollars. You'd blow any savings you make on fuel anyway. The idea of shopping around for fun and profit is to put in the extra effort once every year or two to learn where the best bargains are usually to be found. If you enjoy shopping, then so much the better but the fun in shopping usually lies in getting it over with quickly so you can get back to good times with your friends or family.

Shopping for profit is shopping for savings, quality and value. Buying things that will last will save you megabucks down the track—as the Eighth Law of Gold shows.

HOW TO KNOW IF YOU'RE GETTING VALUE FOR MONEY

For anything that you buy once a year or less, and that costs more than $50, make sure you get three different prices to compare. (If you're struggling, then make it anything over $20, and if you want to be really strict with yourself make it $10.)

You'll know you've got value for money on anything you buy if:

a) you feel good about your purchase a week or two later—shopping instincts are right about 80% of the time or more,

b) you checked three shops and this is either the lowest or second lowest price AND the best or second best quality,

c) you get more than you expected for the same price as elsewhere—like a 20% bigger packet, samples of other products included or free delivery.

Note: Just because something has a sale sticker on it, it does NOT automatically make it good value. Very often prices were inflated to start with and have been dropped just enough to attract your attention to the brightly coloured sticker.

HOW TO GET THE BEST VALUE FROM PEOPLE

Be friendly. Everyone has a hard time making it through some days and a genuinely friendly face now and then often makes it bearable. It also makes shopping more enjoyable for you—and for your wallet as well if they feel generous in return.

Friendliness can really pay off

I once sympathised with a lady who was helping her husband behind the counter of a corner hardware shop. While she tried to serve me a $2 packet of picture-framing nails, he was giving her a really hard time over stocktaking—in particular over garden sheds, of which they seemed to have one too many. If there had been a mistake, there was no way it could have been hers, since she'd only just given up a full-time job and this was her first morning working beside him.

So while he stormed off and ranted at her, she turned to me and asked me where I'd like my free 3m by 3m garden shed delivered.

It was only Zincalume, but I've never heard my lawn-mower complain.

HOW TO BUY THINGS IN OTHER PLACES WITHOUT GOING THERE

Need to compare prices of things outside your area and don't want the STD phone charges? Or too busy to shop around and need to let someone else's fingers do the walking? Or maybe you just want to organise a special gift to be bought and delivered to a friend in another state? Try phoning Telstra's 131SHOP (131 746) for the cost of a local call. Give them your contact details and they'll organise up to three suitable businesses to call you back at their expense. That can save stacks on price hunting and organising holidays out of town. It also saves you time and hassle.

HOW TO BUY CONTENTS FOR YOUR HOUSE

As I suggested in chapter 1, you're old enough to buy furniture as soon as you're old enough to know what you want. And yes, that does mean before you leave high school.

Even if you are one of the few who can afford premium quality furniture the first time round, think about the future. Everything you buy to start with has to survive parties, shifting house a few times, possibly flatmates, and the harshest of tests—little kids—in the first five years or so.

> **Think about what you need. Plan how long you need it to last. And buy everything with these thoughts in mind.**

For example, first time round, go for solid timber or metal furniture, the kind that can be stripped down and repainted or re-covered easily every few years. Tailored cushions are out—unless you're a clever sewer—because they make re-covering costs more expensive, even with the professionals.

Good solid furniture that's easy to makeover will always get you the best resale value later too. If you buy well and care for it, you can practically get 'free' use of it for years by reselling it years later used, for the same price you paid for it now. (That's possibly one of the few upsides of inflation.)

Fabrics for curtains, cushions and carpets should be medium, premium or industrial quality so they last. Avoid pale colours, satins and cottons—which all wear out quickly. *Note:* Lots of 'busy' patterns—that's small tight patterns or clashing combinations of big and small patterns and colours in the one room—are difficult to co-ordinate effectively unless you've got a talent for it. Otherwise they make your house look messy, even if it's clean. And you'll find that you'll get the best resale for anything—even if it's a chair you're selling secondhand—by inviting buyers into a clean, uncluttered home with a pleasant colour scheme.

If you rent or move houses often, choose décor which suits cream wall colours, because even if the walls of your rental house aren't cream, they're likely to be a colour that goes with cream, and if your furniture goes with cream, you've got the best chance of things matching wherever you move. (War between colours in a room tends to encourage war between people.)

Beware of *buy-now-but-don't-pay-anything-until-later* finance offered by many furniture stores. Obviously cash is best. But when you haven't quite saved up enough when that bargain pops up or emergency replacement is needed, consider an overdraft or credit card instead—they're likely to be cheaper in the long run and are certainly more flexible with repayments if something goes wrong.

Furniture tip 1: Keep your eyes on the deceased estate auctions in the newspaper, as elderly people often have quality solid furniture. (And for a small bonus, check any secondhand sofas you buy for hidden treasure after you've paid for them—so any lost coins that have slipped down between cushions are yours. Do it before they're loaded for delivery, however, so they don't fall out in transit.)

HOW TO BUY—WAREHOUSE SHOPPING

Factory outlets, seconds shops and warehouses are both excellent and dangerous at the same time. Warehouse tours teach you where they all are, so you can visit them later at your leisure (if they're open to the general public or perhaps your area may be one of those covered by a 'bargain shoppers' guide' available at newsagencies). But shopping tours can be expensive because you often feel rushed and everyone on the bus gets excited about bargains and buys things they don't really want due to peer pressure. Sometimes there's also coin-eating mini-lotteries run by hosts or guides between each stop—especially if it's a fundraising trip.

Solutions: If you're good with credit and bad with cash, take your credit card and $40 or less—just enough for lunch, lotteries if you're interested, and one or two small splurges. If you're good with cash and bad with credit, take around $80—budgeted out of your sanity allowance, of course—and leave your credit cards at home. If you're dangerous with money no matter how it comes, stay at home.

HOW TO BUY OVER THE INTERNET

To buy anything off the internet, you don't need to be too worried about having to unleash your credit card details through cyberspace. First, choose safe sites—and you can look up each site's security policy before you decide to buy. Credit cards provide a guarantee that only your purchases can be charged to your account. But if you're still not feeling secure, there are sometimes other options:

• You may be able to choose to pay upon receipt of the goods (COD).
• You may be able to pay upon receipt through Australia Post (ring Australia Post for details of companies that have this arrangement or email edeliver@auspost.com.au).
• You may be able to pay over the telephone by credit card by ringing the company directly.
• You may be able to post a cheque or credit card authority in advance of shipment.

Note: Paying by credit card is definitely wiser than paying by cheque or money order, because you can get the goods replaced if they arrive damaged. And you can get your money back if the goods don't arrive at all, or if they're significantly different to what you expected them to be. The Australia Post option is also very safe; however, this is only a new service and some retailers may not have signed up for it yet.

Where internet buying comes into its own is in rare or unusual goods; like collector items or specialist supplies, or in products that haven't been released in our country yet, including new release videos, DVDs and music CDs. In fact it's been said that if you can't find it on the net, then it hasn't been invented yet. (Although sometimes it takes a while to find it.)

Hint: If you want to buy anything over the net—including the best value internet access deals—try using the search engine called *AskJeeves: (*www.askjeeves.com). Instead of keywords, you can ask a proper question like: who has the best deals in CD players? Where can I buy a dining table? What is the lowest price for internet access in my area? Each question will come up with a list of suggestions from companies who have paid to be included.

You can also use this search engine to find Australian search engines—which are often more specialised—by simply asking Jeeves where to find them.

Warning: Until you find out a bit about the company concerned, you are wisest to assume everyone on the net is a crook before committing yourself to any payments, because it's simply too easy to make a disreputable business look reputable on a computer screen. I know eight-year-olds who can do it.

HOW TO BUY MOBILE PHONES

Look at your usage and buy a phone plan that suits it. For example, my mobile phone was mainly for security in case I needed help when I was out. I also planned to divert my home phone to my mobile, so I'd never miss a call when shopping. But the way things worked out, I only use it to make about one call maybe every six months or so, and I have to pull over every time it screams at me when I'm driving. And I can't get reception at the supermarket, or my parents' farm and I'm not allowed to get reception at the cinema or when I'm being interviewed—which doesn't leave too many other opportunities. So unless I ditch the thing altogether, I'm best off with the $5 or $10 a month plan, depending on which features I want on the phone itself—even though it has dearer calls, because I can't get value out of the dearer monthly plans with cheaper calls.

A good friend, however, lives life at the complete opposite end of the scale. He uses his mobile to call other mobiles at least 50 times a day during peak hours. He also uses it to get automatic stock reports messaged to him as well as using it to get email access for his laptop, so he's much better off with a higher monthly rental that's got cheaper call costs and stacks of free calls included in his monthly minimum.

Handy hints: Combining home and mobile accounts and paying them quarterly earns you discounts for having more than one service with the same company as well as keeping your savings for this bill in your bank or mortgage offset account for as long as possible. Also remember: Just because you have a mobile phone for personal security doesn't mean you have to wear the numbers off it by dialling your friends.

Beware of: Hidden charges, accounts that aren't itemised, lengths of calls charged correctly and sneaking in of additional features that you don't use but still have to pay for (like new automatic answering messages.) The standard this-phone-is-either-switched-off-or-not-in-a-network-area message is usually free. Newer or customised messages of the please-leave-a-message-after-the-beep variety may involve fees and if you want to go back to the old free message you have to call them and specifically ask to change it back again. *Note:* When this happened to me recently, I had to ring four times over three months to get it fixed, so I also asked for—and received—all relevant money back.

BIG FUSS OVER NOTHING

Many people have been worried that Telstra's move to give monthly discounts to people who pay their bill over the internet is discrimination against people who can't afford a computer. As the thin end of the wedge, that is something that we—as consumers—will have to keep a suspicious eye on as each company attempts it. But in this case, it's all a big fuss over nothing and I, for one, will not be making any hasty effort to switch to internet bill paying, because:

- Line rental drops from $19.50 to $14.50 per month (saving $5 a month), BUT if you need a hard copy of your account to be posted, it will cost you $3.30. Yes, you can print a legal tax invoice off your screen when you pay, but if your printer is on the blink—as mine usually is when I really need it— you'll have to order one and pay the fee.

- Your local calls will ALL be 19 cents each, instead of 18.5 cents for standard local or 15 cents each for neighbourhood calls. So if you make about 100 neighbourhood calls a month—as many people do—you blow $4 of your $5 savings anyway. (Neighbourhood calls are calls to other numbers on the same telephone exchange as you. See your phonebook for information on telephone prefixes to tell which ones are on your exchange. You'll find it near the centre or back near the listings of postcodes.)

- Logging on to pay your bill will cost you a phone call (19 cents), plus ten to 15 minutes internet time (up to 30 cents), plus printer costs for running off your own statement, plus power for your computer, modem, printer and office light (if you do it at night). All negligible costs by themselves, but you're not chasing much in savings either, are you?

HOW TO SAVE WITH INTERNET SERVICE PROVIDERS (ISPs)

Internet Service Providers are dialled by your computer modem to link your innocent little PC into the staggering— and growing—network of worldwide virtual information.

For ISPs available in your area, check out the classifieds in your local newspaper or library. Ask your friends who they use. And ask small business people that you deal with who they use and what they pay for net access. All ISPs include email in their services, but they have different offers on the size of webpage they can host for your personal interests or business information.

Warning: Ring your home phone provider *before* signing up with any ISP to make sure the number your modem will be dialling will be charged at local calls rates instead of STD.

Handy hints:

- Ask your Internet Service Provider about their censoring services (even if you don't have kids to worry about linking into porno sites by accident). Because by removing the billions of porno sites from your web-search criteria, you can usually find what you're looking for faster, saving you frustration, net time and money.

- If you travel often and require access to your email while you're away, try going for an ISP with server connection phone numbers in every state so you can check your email or send messages to and from any source within Australia.

A DOZEN TIPS FOR BUDGET BRIDES

Here are 12 tips to help make that special day as free of financial pressure and stress as possible.

1. *Budget your date, don't guess it:* Work out your wedding date using sound financial theory:
   - how much—roughly—will your wedding and honeymoon cost?
   - how much can you afford to spend—or save—each pay towards your wedding and honeymoon?
   - using a calendar, work out how many pays you need to save up for everything and then set your date two weeks after that (as a safety net). Or shorten your engagement by having family donate to a garage sale you use to

make money, or by working overtime to afford your wedding sooner. (Don't forget to ring the weather bureau to double-check the mathematical expectation for rain on that day, so you can plan for wedding umbrellas if necessary.)

2. *Get organised:* Get a pocket notebook to record cost comparisons, store business cards and work out your budget.

3. *Cars:* Save up to $1000 by getting friends and family to decorate and drive their favourite cars, or choose your wedding party so you neatly fill a stretch limo, since one big car is cheaper than two or three smaller ones.

4. *Gown:* Save around $2000 by hiring your dress or buying a secondhand gown through local newspapers. It's considered by some to be bad luck to buy a gown from someone whose marriage has failed—or might fail—but you can break the 'hex' by remaking the gown to suit you, adding extra lace, or changing buttons etc.

5. *Suits and bridesmaids' dresses:* Men's suits are nearly as cheap to buy in chainstores as they are to hire. Bridesmaids, however, secretly resent spending money on dresses they can wear publicly only once. So consult your bridesmaids on multi-purpose dress design, or ask if they prefer to hire.

6. *Stationery:* Even supermarkets sell elegant wedding stationery cheaply, but anyone with a PC can print their own personalised invites and place-cards. If you don't have access to a PC, try your local classifieds for someone who advertises a résumé service and offer them a trade on any services that you can provide, eg. washing, ironing or lawnmowing for a week.

See chapter 17: Case Study 3 on page 192 for more hints

7. *Catering:* Halve catering costs by having reliable relatives (aunts, grandparents etc.) bring along the hors d'oeuvres, extra desserts and cakes for supper—making sure your caterer allows this.

8. *Venue:* If married in a church, the church hall is often the cheapest and most convenient place for the reception (also halving costs of hired cars and sometimes caterers), but you must book well ahead, because everyone who gets married that day will want to get it first. Otherwise, try a leafy backyard with BBQ tables and chairs borrowed from friends and family. Spray-paint the rubbish bins in colours to suit your bridesmaids' outfits for a cheap but memorable touch.

9. *Entertainment:* A hall with a built-in stereo is often cheaper than a DJ. Just put a reliable friend or relative in charge of guarding and playing your CDs. A park with an adjoining playground is also a great distraction for little kids and tipsy groomsmen.

10. *Grog:* Some pubs will buy back unopened alcohol and provide or rent glasses, but fees on breakages can be expensive. Ask first, before you order.

11. *Little splurges on little extras:* Guests remember weddings best when they get thoughtful little extras to enjoy. A cheap favourite is three sugared almonds tied in a 10cm square of netting with a tiny ribbon to match your bridesmaids' outfits. Count your almonds before you buy, so you don't over-cater. ($30 to $40 caters for 60–80 guests.)

12. *Flowers: fake or fresh?* Fresh are elegant but short-lived, expensive and a last minute hassle on the day. Fake flowers are cheaper and can be bought as soon as you can afford them. For example, I bought 10m of ribbon for $10 and six big bunches of fake flowers from the supermarket for $30— white chrysanthemums which I coloured as required. I pulled apart the bunches and re-arranged them to make a trailing bridal bouquet (which I later sold for $40), three big bunches for my bridesmaids to keep, flower combs for our hair, pockets for my groomsmen and both sets of parents, and two arrangements for the cake table. I did it all three months before the wedding, leaving nothing to worry about on the day—and I'd never done flower-arranging

before. There are plenty of books available—try your local library—to tell you how to do it.

HOLIDAY TIPS: SEEING THE WORLD ON A SHOE-STRING

Warning: Holidays away from home are a reward, not a right. The tips that follow are therefore intended only for people who have sorted out their pressing financial problems, not those who want to escape them.

Please do not misinterpret this. I DO NOT suggest that only rich people deserve holidays. I DO suggest that people who haven't paid their bills before going away may have their priorities warped.

Holidays are a reward for a hard year's slog at work. It's time off to rest and recuperate so you can get back into it again—this time with a smile on your face.

Sure, they can be short. Sometimes all you need is a naughty night away from the kids at a hotel with your sweetheart. Or a week off now and then to enjoy the house and family you work so hard to support. But once every three to five years, you really need to get away—a complete change of scenery to recharge the old think-tank and fill up with fresh inspiration.

Get the best value from money-hungry holidays by stretching the moment as well as your dollar.

STRETCHING THE MOMENT

- Exotic holidays start at home—with planning. The longer you plan, the longer the holiday excitement seems to last. Collect free brochures from travel agents: up to two years before an overseas holiday, and up to 12 months before a trip inside Australia. Leave them in the loo, your bedroom and lounge room to drool over.
- Wrap pictures of your destination around homebrand canned foods with rubber bands, so budget cutbacks remind you of your goal every time you open the fridge or cupboard.

- Keep calendars in the kitchen, loo and two other popular rooms with a countdown of 'number of sleeps left before holidays' marked in red.
- Work extra hard before you nip off for an official bludge, and every second you're on holiday will taste sweeter.

Exotic holidays are money-hungry. Stretch your dollar by trying one of the following: (All costs are in Australian dollars, unless otherwise stated.)

HOUSE-SWAPPING (IN OR OUT OF AUSTRALIA)
Pros: Does away with hotel, restaurant and car rental costs and having to find someone to feed Fido.
Cons: Someone else has access to your undie drawer and perhaps learns Aussie road rules in your car.
Note: It's customary to arrange neighbours or family to introduce your house-swappers to your rottweiler, TV remote and local shops, and also to keep an eye on them.

Register your house for swapping internationally on as many websites as you wish, but beware of listing charges or annual fees which are generally around $20 to $60. You'll need to email or post a photo of your house to the house-swapping registry and provide details of how many rooms it has and what kind of facilities or tourist attractions are close. And yes, it is for any netsurfers to see, but you usually have a say in who gets access to your personal contact details—the choice being anyone who hits your site, or only registered users.

Some websites specialise in particular countries, but whoever you choose, I suggest emailing a handful of people who have already paid to be registered—and who have made their contact details available for anyone—to see if they think the service is worthwhile BEFORE you post off a cheque.

Websites are countless, but interesting ones I've seen include: www.ultranet.com, www.digsville.com and sunswap.com.au.

To prevent serious disappointment and expense on any house-swapping scheme, I also suggest getting additional photos posted to you directly, showing the owners doing things both inside and outside the house before making final arrangements, just in case they've slipped in photos of a house from a magazine or maybe one of their neighbours' houses down the street. To be doubly cautious, return the photos to the house's address *without* the people's name on the front. Make sure you include a note saying that if these photos have not been provided with the owners' consent, please contact you immediately to prevent you from showing up on their doorstep by mistake. To be triply cautious, if travelling overseas, you could always post copies of the photos with a stamped and self-addressed envelope to an address at random close to the one you're interested in, asking them to verify that this is the house at this address. (Or you could get into an internet chatroom, do a search for someone from that area, scan and e-post the photo to them and ask them to check personally and get back to you. People in chatrooms are usually extremely friendly and helpful.)

For holidays inside Australia, don't forget the option of house-swapping or visiting with far-flung cousins, aunts or uncles, or their neighbours.

HOSTING EXCHANGE STUDENTS

Be a host family for exchange students—three weeks a year each. Then visit them in their countries where you should get free accommodation and tour guides! Cost: meals and room for them in your house, plus travel to their country. Contact: Youth For Understanding 1800 654 947 or website: www.yfu.com.au.

Don't host exchange students *just* because of possible savings on overseas holidays.

Host students to make your life richer. Any dollar savings later are a happy bonus.

FLYING BY THE BACKSIDE OF YOUR BRITCHES

Round-trip tickets overseas—starting at around $1500 to England for example—are usually cheaper than one-way tickets bought in Australia. They're also a good defence for uptight immigration officials, especially at London's Heathrow and Gatwick airports. But England has cheap flights to Australia—as low as $400—so consider a one-way ticket to say, Amsterdam $870—where officials are more relaxed—with a bus or train ticket to the next country in your pocket, just in case they ask.

London also often has cheap airfares to Barcelona, Munich, Rome and Athens. Dirt cheap seats are sold first, so book in advance. Flights without meals are cheaper again if available.

Make sure dates for your flights can be changed without hassle or extra cost.

When flying out of Oz or NZ, make the most of stopovers in Indonesia, Singapore or Thailand. Consider getting tailor-made clothing including business-wear dirt cheap (especially in Bangkok) on your way.

Always check arrival times and 24-hour services at airports. Some airports are closed after hours or have no comfy sofas, which is a hassle and expensive for getting to hotels/hostels by taxi if public transport has stopped for the night.

BACKPACKING WITH OR WITHOUT THE BACKPACK

Travel before your 26th birthday and you're eligible for backpacker discounts around the world for travel and accommodation. Yes, even if you're not a backpacker. Or join Youth Hostels Australia at any age on (02) 9261 1111 or website: www.yha.com.au for discounts on everything, even for families. Membership is about $49 or $15 if you're under 18.

Sample cost for hostels per night: India $4, USA $16, UK $26.

TRAINS AND BUSES

Busabout and Eurolines are often the best value travel passes in Europe, but they don't have the flexibility of some other rail passes. Costs are around $500 to $1800.

Trains are often the best way to get around Europe. They're roomy, go everywhere and leave hourly to most European destinations. Save on bus/taxis by getting a train into the centre of town instead of flying into the outskirts.

Beware of expensive hitches like 'supplements' on fare tickets, a bit like compulsory tipping. (Italian train supplements can add up to 30% extra!) In many countries, trains which require supplements are in red on timetables.

- Always stock up on supermarket food and wine beforehand as train food costs a fortune.

- In Italy, pay a little extra for train reservations, or be prepared to stand up for three hours or more on busy routes.

- Make the most of rail passes with limited days (eg. Eurail Flexipass) by using it only in more expensive countries, like the Scandinavian countries, France, Belgium, the Netherlands, Germany, Switzerland and Austria. Trains are cheapest in Italy and eastern Europe. In Germany, Deutsche Bahn's Happy Weekend Tickets are usually cheaper than your pass.

CARS AND BIKES

For long trips in Europe with groups of friends, consider buying a share car in London, where registration and insurance are often cheaper and forms are in English. (*Beware:* In cities, parking can be a pain as well as expensive!)

Try the car market on Market Street, near the Caledonian Road tube station, or check out UK magazines *Auto Trader* and *Loot*. Or try *J'Annonce* in France. Then sell the car again quickly the same way before you come home. Prices start around $200 for a Morris four-door auto.

If you are spending 70% or more of your time in continental Europe, buy a car there, because while England,

Scotland, Wales, Ireland, the Channel Islands, the Isle of Man, Cyprus and Malta drive on the left with the steering wheel on the right, everywhere else has the steering wheel on the left. Ask friends or relatives in Europe to register and insure cars in their names to save big dollars. (*Note:* Foreigners can't own cars in the Netherlands.)

OR . . . put in with friends to share a Eurodrive 17-day to 6-month lease with roadside assistance from Renault for big savings and less worries.

If renting a car or bike, get a better deal by hiring them in the various regions, using them only locally, then taking the bus/train between towns.

CRUISING THE BLUE

For budget travel to a specific destination, forget a cruise ship. Flying is faster at a fraction of the price, giving you more time to spend hanging from a cliff in the Andes or crisping on the beaches in Vanuatu. Yes, cruiseliners stop over at exotic locations, but mainly it's the trip that's the adventure. Prices usually include accommodation, meals and entertainment at sea, so remember that when comparing prices to other methods of travel. Overall, if the destination doesn't matter, sailing the ocean blue can be great value for a package holiday. Sample cost: a nine-night South Pacific cruise to three ports for a family of four people starts at $1070 for a share cabin on the lower decks.

HOW NOT TO PAY FOR HOLIDAYS

- DON'T pay for holidays with a personal loan. You spend years paying them off, when you could be going on more holidays.
- DON'T forget to weigh up the cost of income lost by taking leave without pay to travel interstate or overseas. (Eg. if you could have earned $2000 while you were off spending $3000 in Bali, the true cost of your holiday is $5000.)
- DO put $20 to $30 a week into a goal savings account for at

least a year before each overseas holiday.

- DO use credit cards to pay your bookings in advance. Then ring the airport/bus/train and confirm your ticket is reserved. If not, ring your bank and cancel the charge and dob in the dodgy agent. Also, if the airline, hotel or travel agent goes bust, you can get your money back through your bank.
- DO use your goal savings account to pay your credit card out before you leave. An empty credit card on holidays is a must to be able to take advantage of unexpected bargains.

15

Give Yourself a Money Makeover

WHAT IS A MONEY MAKEOVER?
Since the launch of my first book, I've frequently been given the gigantic task of working through a broad selection of budgets so I can demonstrate—usually on camera—how simple and easy certain budgeting strategies can be.

Working through people's budgets like this is the financial equivalent of giving them a personal makeover. It's a whole new look that makes you feel better about yourself; thus they've come to be affectionately known as money makeovers. (The Radical Case Studies in chapter 17, are a sample of the makeovers that I've done.)

And no, I don't charge anything for doing them. But it's not something I have time to do very often because it takes me two to four long days to do each one—not because they're difficult, but because I have to get inside the family's life through long phone calls and photographs to see what they're doing wrong before I can investigate options available in their suburb to fix their problems.

Don't get me wrong, I *love* doing it. I love playing with money and showing people how exciting money management can be. But I simply don't have enough time to help very many people individually. It's much easier—and much better for you in the long run—for me to teach you how to do it for yourself.

That's also because nothing I can do for you is anything comparable to what you can do for yourselves. For instance, as incredible as these makeovers seem, they're only the smallest tip of the financial iceberg. There are still stacks more things that each of these families can do, now that they understand the possibilities that have been opened up to them.

After reading this book, in less time than it takes to scoff a coffee and a Tim Tam, you should be able to spot around $100 to $300 every fortnight in savings too.

This chapter helps you pull what you've read from other chapters into a focused 12-step guide to putting your new knowledge into action, by starting you off to fix the most common mistakes.

HOW TO GIVE YOURSELF A MONEY MAKEOVER

Step 1: Read chapter 4 if you haven't already done so and work out your budget as shown.

Step 2: Write down exactly what your immediate financial needs are. If you have trouble figuring out how to start, just pretend I'm the Money Santa. I've just rung you to tell you that I'll pay the next $1000 worth of your bills for you, and you can spend the savings on anything you really need *if* you can tell me in 50 words or less what it is you need before I hang up. What would you ask for?

If you're stuck for ideas—and I'd be really surprised if you are—just flip to chapter 17: Radical Case Studies and read up on what other people have needed. Or jot down any big outstanding bills or big bills that you know you've got coming that you really wish would disappear.

Step 3: Write down the words CONTENTS INSUR-ANCE—especially if you're renting—even if you're already paying it. (*Note:* If you're paying off your mortgage you should already have building insurance, as it's required by most loans, but if you don't, then add building insurance to your list as well.)

If you don't already pay contents insurance, you're about to—step 1 should have shown you if there's room already in your budget, and if not, I'll show you how to make room.

The lower your income, the more important it becomes to insure your belongings against loss—especially if you live in a high crime area. You can't stay financially successful for long on a low income if someone else can break in and steal it all away from you.

If you do already pay this type of insurance, then ring around now and make sure you're getting the best deal—where *cheapest* does not necessarily mean *best*. (Look for level of cover and compare policies for the fewest exclusions and excesses.) If you're still unconvinced, then imagine for a second what you'd do if your house burned down and you had to replace everything and still had to finish paying off furniture and other things that you didn't have anymore.

Same goes for car insurance. If you can't survive without your car, then insure it if it's worth insuring or start a savings account to replace it with another cheapie if you lose it.

Ring any three to five of the major insurance companies for quotes on how much it will cost you per pay and at the same time ask them if they accept weekly or monthly payments or only annual ones. Don't pay monthly if it's cheaper to pay annually. Park the money in your credit card until you need it and save on interest.

> **Failing to insure your important belongings is like sticking a sign on your back that says 'kick me please'.**

While you're on the line—which is only a local call—take the opportunity to get quotes for combining any of your other insurances all into one policy: including house, contents, car, CTP (from your rego) and health, boat or travel insurance. Write down how much you'll save by changing or combining policies and circle this as potential savings. *Note:* Strangely, individual insurances with various companies are often cheaper than bulk packages.

If you weren't already paying contents insurance, write down how much you have to budget each pay to pay for it. Contents policies are usually only $5 to $10 a fortnight—that's cheap peace of mind that you deserve.

Step 4: Circle all the other obvious places in which you can cut back without upsetting anyone in the family too much. I'm assuming your budget is in a fairly tragic state right now, so suggestions include the most common little splurges: takeaway meals and trips to the cinema. Cancel regular mail order subscriptions (including collector sets of plates or spoons or whatever that you may be buying over a period of time) and magazine subscriptions; memberships you don't get much use out of; and cut back on or cancel newspaper deliveries. (If you really want to keep getting a newspaper, check out its subscription offers. Many papers will home deliver at a cost of up to $100 a year cheaper than the cover price, and payments can be made monthly.)

Step 5: If you've paid out your car loan or house loans, ring to make sure the insurers have been told, so you're being charged at a discounted rate.

Step 6: Ring your home and mobile phone service providers and see if you're on the best plan for your usage. Special offers change with annoying regularity—and you're not always automatically eligible for them; you often have to ask for them by phone. But you *can* often get decent discounts if you combine bills onto one account—and keep your eyes on your junk mail for ads on special deals.

Step 7: If you have a mortgage, now's a good time to do a quick check to see if you're getting the best deal, and if you're not, to figure out if it's really worth changing all your banking in order to change. If you're not confident to do this calculation by yourself, check the relevant section in my previous book or else ring a mortgage broker and ask for a 'mortgage health check'. Make sure it's a free service though, and if you do decide to change loans, make sure they'll do everything for you at no cost to you (because the bank you choose will pay them a commission. On that point, make sure the mortgage broker gets the same commission scale from every bank, no matter who you choose, so you have some reassurance that you're not being herded towards the one that pays them the biggest kickback.) The only national mortgage broker that I know of who fulfils all of these criteria is Mortgage Choice, but certainly look around as there may be other suitable state-based brokers out there.

Step 8: If you or any member of your family is unable to work because of some kind of debilitating or ongoing health problem, then check out Pennies from Heaven in the Appendix to see if you're eligible for a disability pension or medical benefits.

Step 9: If you're a family with children ring Centrelink. Explain your situation and ask them to double-check that you're being paid the right amount of family and other allowances.

Step 10: Get a copy of the latest Tax Pack free from most newsagencies or from the Tax Office (phone 13 28 61) and read the explanation of every deduction in the deduction questions. This will very quickly tell you if you've been claiming everything you're allowed to, and it will also clue you in on things you can legally claim for next year—provided legislation doesn't change. Donations of used clothes and furniture, for instance, can be claimed as deductions if you get a receipt for their approximate value.

Step 11: Try to limit your opportunities to spend money. For a list of suggestions on how to stop yourself from opening your wallet, check out the next chapter of case studies.

Step 12: Lower your living standards—yeah, I know you don't like that one. But I have to include it, because you'd be surprised how many people try to live a BMW lifestyle on a Barina budget. Besides, it's not a life sentence—it's just a short-term solution for solving your budget dilemmas.

WHAT CAN WE DO?
(QUICK QUESTIONS ANSWERED)

Here's some of the most common questions that people ask me when I'm helping them through their makeovers:

POCKETMONEY FOR THE KIDS

I have three children and I'd love to be able to buy them treats, but I can't afford them. What can we do?

Plenty. Kids are really bright these days. Sit them down and work out what they want and how much it's going to cost. Put an IOU on the fridge that gets checked off with all the chores they do which release your time for income-producing hobbies like childminding, housekeeping etc. Then pay your kids when you get paid.

THE UNCO-OPERATIVE SPOUSE

My hubby and I are always fighting over money. He spends it down the boozer and I want to save. What can I do?

Not much. Budget commitments must be a joint decision. You can do a lot by yourself, but not all. Once you've started, once you've got your home loan dropping by thousands every month and your nest-egg growing with every paypacket, it's much easier to motivate your partner—I know. But in the meantime, it's a hard slog for you. Remember, he's quite within his rights to spend his sanity allowance every pay, in any way he chooses—just as you can. It's the size of that sanity allowance that could be the problem.

NEED CASH FAST

My credit card debts are out of control. What can I do?

Stop spending money for one thing! Then work out a budget to pay off the rest. Have a garage sale, take up a paying hobby, change jobs to cash in your holiday pay, trade down to a less trendy but still reliable car, or do overtime to pay it off. There's actually stacks you can do. You've done your crime. Now do your time.

16

The Fast $5000 Rescue Package

For emergencies only!!! This chapter shows how almost any low-income earner can find $5000 to $35,000 fast in order to wipe their debts and then start again with a clean slate by going back to chapter 2. I put this chapter at the back of this book because you shouldn't have to do these things unless you're close to bankruptcy. Please use these suggestions as a last resort only. They unlock your 'buried' assets and strip your resources to the bone, leaving you vulnerable for a short time until you rebuild your life and your budget.

> **You don't have to do everything listed. Just use what you need.**

Note: Many of these tips are safe to use for raising a deposit for a house, but only because you won't actually be spending the money, you'll simply be converting it into part of a solid investment.

Also please note that if you're a first home buyer, you might as well call this the *Fast $15,000 Rescue Package*, because $5000 is a conservative figure and you blast that into the weeds in one step with the $7000 First Home Owner Grant ($14,000 if you're building from 9 March 2001 to 31 December 2001).

Do not use these tips for non-essential purchases or holidays!

TRADE JOBS—$1500 TO $2500

They say a change is as good as a holiday, so put an average of $1500 to $2500 into your pocket by planning a job change—if possible—instead of taking four weeks off as a holiday. No, you can't do this every year, because you'll burn yourself out and drive your family insane.

In most cases, you're entitled to four weeks' holiday every year. And the less time you take off between jobs, the more of your lump sum holiday pay you get to spend as a bonus.

If you're worried that your boss might not pay out your holiday pay—which is possible, even though it is illegal—then just ask to be paid your holiday pay without telling them you're leaving. Hand in your notice—once your holiday cheque has cleared—to be effective from the *last* day of your holidays. That should officially give them enough notice to find a replacement, and they'll still have to pay you a small severance pay for the holidays that accrue while you're on holidays. (This is because you're still accruing holidays while you're on holidays. For example, if you get four weeks' holiday pay a year, that's about 1.5 days' pay that you should get if you resigned at the end of your holidays. Actually, the majority of Australians tend to have more than four weeks' holiday owing to them at any time, so it's likely that you could be entitled to more than $2500.)

'Borrow' a small amount from your holiday pay to tide you over until you get your first pay in the new job, and then pay it back to use the full bonus towards your rescue package. Naturally this strategy only works if you have another job to go to straight away, so organise it in advance.

$1000 BONUS FOR TRADING JOBS

Some superannuation funds give you the option of a lump sum payout on the contributions that you arranged to have *taken out of your paypacket* while you were working (sometimes there's an age limit). If you've been working for more than a year, that's usually worth over $1000. (*Note:* You can't take out the preserved benefit portion that your employer put in—only your own contributions.)

EXTRA $5000 BONUS TO TRADING JOBS

If you've been working for more than ten years you'll also be due long-service leave under most awards, usually worth more than $5000.

LIFE INSURANCE—$2000 TO $15,000

Some policies allow you to borrow the money that you've put in so far—sometimes for a small fee. (Sometimes the fee is built into your premiums on the assumption that you'll be doing this!) Depending on the policy, you can either arrange higher regular payments to catch up again, or you can agree to reduced cover—or a combination.

There's usually a minimum amount you can withdraw, and you won't be allowed to withdraw the total of your contributions, but for someone who's been contributing for a decade or so you should have between $2000 and $15,000 available if you really need it. Contact your insurance company to find out the full flexibility of your policy.

SUPERANNUATION—UP TO $100 A MONTH

You can't access any of your contributions and you can't access the interest that's been paid so far, but if you are in one of the categories of jobs with compulsory personal contributions, you can sometimes apply for a reduced percentage of those to be deducted from your paypacket if you're suffering financial hardship. Ask your pay officer or ring the fund directly for details and an application. (*Note:* I'm not talking about the compulsory superannuation that your employer has to pay for you.)

TRADE CARS—$2500 TO $10,500

Unless you *really* love your car, consider selling it for a cheaper but still reliable set of wheels to use the difference as a deposit.

Note: I did the opposite and got similar savings. For example, while still struggling financially, I traded two secondhand, expensive-to-run cars for a brand new, economical car which also halved rego, insurance and running costs.

Or you could try selling your partner's car and carpool with them, so you not only get a decent bonus for your rescue package, you also get more time together while you're travelling to work.

Changing your car(s) for other car(s)—either higher or lower in value—can:

- get you a bonus which seems to fall between $2000 and $10,000 for most low-income earners;
- make travelling cheaper usually by about $500 a year while you get your budget back under control;
- eliminate at least one car loan that might also be preventing you from getting a home loan.

HOLD A CAR-BOOT OR GARAGE SALE—$500 TO $2000

Out with everything you don't really want or need—starting with the long white dress that's probably sitting in the back of your wardrobe. If, on the other hand, you're about to get married, you've got a good excuse to ask all your friends and relatives to donate goods or a percentage of their goods to your sale too—and help you out on the day—perhaps as a new-fashioned 'bridal shower'.

Ask them to clean out their spare rooms and plan to run the sale for two weekends in a row. Keep a guard on the gate and a few around the yard so goods don't walk. Price everything so you don't get bugged with questions all day. Hang balloons or blown-up kitchen gloves or condoms on the letterbox to attract attention. Be prepared to say no to hagglers. (Some second-hand dealers have made it an art form—some even dress down their appearance so you'll take pity on them, thinking they're worse off than you are. If hagglers start to get annoying, simply ask them to leave.) Make extra bucks by selling hot dogs and cold drinks in the backyard at $2 each. (Buy warm drink cans cheap from the supermarket to chill and resell). One friend made over $600 this way in one day at her joint-family garage sale! Use the word *bric-a-brac* in your ads—that means lots of interesting knick-knacks.

Bottom line: Your average, well-organised garage sale can make you $500 to $2000.

17

Radical Case Studies

The following case studies highlight some fairly radical, unorthodox, and sometimes downright brazen things that you can do to resurrect a blown-out budget without having to live on bread and water or become a social leper in the process. They were done—free of charge to the people involved—to help promote *Your Mortgage and How to Pay it off in Five Years* either as part of current affairs television programs or as part of special features that I wrote for various women's magazines. They are *not* the most extreme examples. In fact they're fairly typical of the kinds of problems that are being suffered by all kinds of people around the country.

> **Note:** The stories, facts and figures in this chapter are all true—only the names have been changed to protect the guilty!

CASE STUDY 1: The Layby Queen
The problem: *Sandy is a secretary and a self-confessed shopaholic. She wants to go to England but doesn't have the money because ever since she earned her first pay she's been 'obsessed' with buying things. At first it was only during grocery shopping, but now, even if it's just a pair of*

knickers during her lunchbreak, she just has *to buy something whenever she's out. She's had the phone cut off more than once for missing payments, and she was even forced to live on flour, water, peas and rice for a month! But Sandy earns a decent wage. Her living expenses eat only half of it, then she blows the rest—$400 every fortnight—on things she doesn't really want or need. She has no credit card, but is a layby queen, and her problem is compounded by friends who encourage her spending. Her lack of self-esteem also leaves her prey to common sales' tricks like store staff suggesting she 'couldn't afford it anyway.'*

Sandy is not alone. Around the planet, everyone with money in their wallet is being encouraged by governments, banks and retailers to spend it again. We need their services to keep us from reverting to the realm of cave-dwellers, so we're happy to go along with them. Problems can arise because most of us suffer to some degree from two basic desires: to improve our lifestyles, and to show the world that we are worth something. Unfortunately for our wallets, buying things can satisfy both of those needs.

The solution: Sandy quite rightly wants to buy things with which to spoil herself after her living expenses are paid. She's just being tricked into renting things or buying the wrong things; things that don't build wealth or make her feel better about herself in the long run.

The 'right' outlays for her money might include pubbing it with friends only once or twice a week instead of six, a new television, a block of land, a superannuation fund for her old age, or the sponsorship of a third-world child. The choice is hers.

But she does want to go to England next year and she needs about $8000 to do it. So the first thing she has to do is start saving $300 every single pay for the next 26 fortnights!

That's one heck of a chunk out of her disposable income, but to meet the goal she's set for herself that's what it's going to take.

In the meantime, she needs to do something radical. After seven pays, when she's got $2100 saved, she could try what I did to improve her self-esteem: ring a stockbroker and buy a minimum parcel of shares in her favourite chainstores. Then she'll feel like THEIR boss for a change and everywhere she goes, she can point at shops and say to herself, 'Hey, I own that!' She may also find—as I did—that she won't want to buy things off the shelf so much anymore, because in a way, she owns everything on the shelf already!

I would also pity the next snobby salesperson who tries to sucker her into a sale with the line, 'It's obviously more than you can afford, my dear,' because Sandy can just smile sweetly and say, 'Look honey, I'm a shareholder and I don't like the way you're treating our customers.' Then walk out.

Also—while she's saving—Sandy needs to tell all her budget-blowing friends where to get off. She's going to *England!* This is a major life experience here, something she has to work hard towards. If friends don't support her, then they're no real friends at all. And those who are her friends should remind her of her goals if she asks to borrow money, then if that fails they should tease her and make a game of it by threatening to write 'budget-blower' on her forehead. Anything to support her.

And if Sandy is still tempted to spend whenever she's out, then she shouldn't go out. Instead she should grocery shop once a fortnight, at night when she's tired. She should wear uncomfortable shoes, or daggy clothes so she just wants to get home. She should not leave her workplace or a nearby park at lunchtime. Instead she should pack a lunch and read about England. If she can, she should work overtime at night, or cut a deal with the boss to work through lunchbreaks and go home early. Then she should go straight home, do not pass you-know-what and do not spend $200!

It's great that Sandy doesn't have a credit card. But layby is just the flipside of the plastic. In my dictionary they mean the same: buy now what you can't afford and figure out how to pay for it later.

Other tips for Sandy and over-eager shoppers like her are to never carry more than $20 (and a phonecard) in your wallet—

just enough to be safe. If you don't have it, you can't spend it. Then make a list of all the things you really *do* want to buy for yourself or for friends with the amount left over after you've saved for your primary goal. And start working down the list.

Every pay you *ARE* going to buy something special for yourself, but you're going to decide what it is before you go out, and you're going to go to up to six different places to compare prices. When you've found your best price, then you're going to go back and get it. And if salespeople give you that 'surely you can't afford that' look, just smile and turn your back, because their shops are in debt to the rafters. They *need* your money. But you, my friend, can shop anywhere you want.

If you're a shopaholic, stuff your purse with nasties: a man's g-string, a few colourful condoms, a dirty tissue or a dead spider . . . anything that will make you embarrassed to open it in public.

CASE STUDY 2: THE EXPECTANT COUPLE

The problem: *Carey and her husband, Joe, are teachers, each earning $50,000 pa, but in a few months Carey will start maternity leave for their first child. The first six weeks are on full pay, the next six weeks on half pay, and the rest of the year is without pay. Their goals are to survive on one wage with their mortgage and new baby until Carey returns to work, and then to move to a bigger house as soon as they can afford it. They were steaming ahead with an early home ownership goal by paying $1115.00/fn into their mortgage offset account, but plan to revert to their standard $615/fn while Carey is on leave.*

The solution: This couple has four big things to look at: mortgage repayments, income tax, government allowances and budgeting.

Mortgage repayments: Carey and Joe were already getting monthly statements—a good thing, since regular reminders help to keep you focused on the problem. So I asked Carey to look at how much interest they had paid in their last month.

Then we divided that amount by how many days were in the month and discovered they were paying $22 a day! So I suggested that instead of dropping back to their standard $615 per fortnight, they add on two days worth of interest and pay $659 instead. This is still affordable on their one wage, but it means that if their debt was an ocean, they'd be dog-paddling towards shore instead of just barely treading water in their baby's first year. And they can drop the repayment if they ever do get into trouble or need a little extra cash in the meantime.

Income tax: Carey's wage runs out about three pays before the end of the financial year, but income tax is deducted from pays on the assumption that we work for a full year. So if it's been a pretty normal year for her, she can look forward to a nice refund. Rocket that claim in, Carey!

(Also, since she returns to work a few months before the end of the following financial year, she should get a good percentage of her tax back that year too. That's nice to look forward to, but won't help her much now when she really needs it.)

Government allowances: I reminded Carey to make sure the maternity nurse gives her the claim forms for family allowances BEFORE she leaves hospital. That way she can post them off and get the government maternity payment and fortnightly family allowances paid within a few weeks. (Late applications don't get backpaid to the date of birth.)

Budgeting: Between the day you discover there was a hole in your condom and the day you say goodbye to workmates for a while, there's only about 16 fortnightly pays with which to flog your budget. That means you should be squirrelling away between $10 and $50 a pay into a savings account for spending later on little bumpkins. Or you can try stockpiling. Aside from baby clothes and maternity consumables like wet ones, cotton buds and disposable nappies (for after the first month), maternity modess and super-soft nipple pads, consider stashing away washing detergents, toilet paper, tinned vegetables—even tinned petfood, if you've got four-legged furry friends—just as if you're preparing for a year-long mini-holocaust!

When Carey's wage drops to half pay, I suggest they practise living entirely off Joe's wage. They'd have to do it soon anyway, so they might as well try with her half pay as a safety net. They could put it in their mortgage offset account along with the money they already put aside for paying bills.

On two wages, this bill savings account was coping nicely, but the added boost will help get them through baby's first Christmas and all those other accounts that just love to pop in at the same time.

And breastfeed. No matter what else you might think, formula feeding—unless it's a physical necessity—is not an option for the budget-conscious. It's expensive with a capital E. Disposable nappies, however, are much of a muchness compared to cloth nappies once you've counted initial costs and washing. Remember, your time now is more valuable than ever. If it's not spent with baby, you should be resting.

Keep your eyes open for sales. Garage sales are nice places for GST avoidance as well as a pace change, but remember to sterilise anything secondhand if it's for bumpkins. For cheap—but quality—maternity clothes, I recommend op shops, community noticeboards, and mothers' groups, which you'll find wherever you can count more than 12 youngsters in one place; like kindergartens, childcare centres and preschools. You can also socialise cheaply at their playgroups and babyclubs.

These mothers' groups are all great places for buying secondhand toys and baby furniture too, so don't be afraid to make contact, long before bumpkins is old enough to join.

Babyclubs run by pharmacies are a little different, providing free health and nutrition advice and many free samples in exchange for your name on their mailing list—and you can join these while you've still got your flat belly.

CASE STUDY 3: WEDDING BELLS

The problem: *Jessie is a 21-year-old apprentice chef, earning only $20,000 a year in the hand. Her fiancé, Ken, lost his permanent job in the week they moved into their new home and now makes their $200 a* *week mortgage repayment from his casual wage, while Jessie spends her pay on the couple's bills and groceries. They own their own car, plus two 'partial' others, which Ken is in the process of 'doing up'. They don't have any pets, furniture, loans or credit cards and their next major financial goal is to get married in six months' time.*

This couple is already extremely careful with money. Jessie keeps her grocery bill down to an amazing $50 a week by budgeting carefully. Her 'crafty' mother helps out making curtains etc. around the home. And they still have about $70 every week to blow on hobbies and entertainment.

Having worked very hard for the last two years, Jessie and Ken have also managed to buy their first home and put about $3000 aside for bills and savings in a mortgage offset account. This means that the interest on their home loan isn't calculated on how much they owe. It's calculated on how much they owe MINUS how much they have in their offset account. And that will save them thousands in interest over the term of their loan.

At the time they applied for the loan, the bank actively encouraged them to splurge on furniture and other home improvements. But this cautious couple realised they were just being encouraged to buy, buy, buy—and figure out how to pay for it later! So they cleverly avoided the offer. They also chose to avoid the revolving credit scheme that's available with this type of loan, by NOT buying things on credit card at all. That's a personal choice that won't affect them too much, but there's still quite a few things they can do to improve their financial situation, in ways that will protect them if things go wrong.

The solution: Firstly, since Ken's mechanical tinkering keeps him happy and fits nicely in their budget, he should keep it up. Had you worried, did I guys? No, you don't have to give up your favourite hobbies. In fact, and particularly when you're unemployed, hobbies are vital to fighting off the dole-queue blues and the soul-crushing feelings of inadequacy. Also, a busy, happy partner is a vital ingredient for financially successful young couples; and if he intends to keep the cars once they're properly roadworthy, they are a handy financial safety net, since they can be sold if something goes wrong and money gets really tight.

Next, because he works only casually, it can be dangerous for the couple to rely on his wage to make the house repayments. If his pay is short one week, then they'll have to make up the difference manually out of Jessie's wage or from their mortgage offset savings. Otherwise they will fall behind and could also be penalised with hefty bank fees and charges.

Instead, this couple might consider devoting Jessie's more reliable wage to making the loan repayments, leaving her with $180 for groceries, wedding plans, and a small sanity allowance to spoil herself with every pay.

Ken's wage can then be devoted to the couple's bill paying account (kept in the mortgage offset account) and his small sanity allowance, which he'll either blow at the canteen at work or save up to spend on his cars, perhaps.

I also suggest that he should still make a small contribution to the loan repayments—on top of the standard repayment that Jessie makes. His 'bit' should be as much or as little as they could afford—even if it's just $5—and will depend on how many hours he gets paid for that week. This way, they are still hammering away at that big fat principal debt that's hanging over their heads and marching their way closer to financial freedom. Also, budgeting like this will help to protect them if one or more of Ken's casual pays falls short, since their bill paying account is already ahead and they won't notice a delay in its regular top-ups.

They also need to get monthly loan statements (if they can get them from their bank without being charged extra fees). Because, although scary at first, these monthly reminders help to keep the problem in front of their faces, motivate them to tackle their debt, and reward them with proof that they are actually getting somewhere when they make those extra repayments.

For example, every extra $10.80 a week that this couple can commit to extra repayments at this stage in their loan will slash one whole year off the term of their mortgage imprisonment!

How's that for motivation? Not so hard to slash ten bucks from the weekly budget when you can see what a massive impact it has, hmm?

Ken should remember that thought when he goes back to working full-time. Because if he can 'up' his repayment contributions to $285 a week, while Jessie is still paying the standard repayments, this couple will have that whopping $100,000 debt completely gone in five incredible years. That's debt-free, while they're still in their twenties!

In the meantime, the couple has got that special day in spring to budget for. That's only 26 pays away. So even though Jessie has got clever friends and relatives who might help her with dresses, decorations and the cake, she still needs to start hoarding like a packrat. Wine, shoes, jewellery, invitations, sexy underthingies, table decorations and artificial flowers can all be bought a little at a time and stockpiled. She should budget at least $50 every pay if she can, not forgetting to allow savings for their honeymoon. The last thing they want is to start married life together with an unexpected debt, and by using the tips for budget brides in the previous chapter, they can save up to $5000.

CASE STUDY 4: SINGLE INCOME FAMILY, RENTING, WITH MAJOR DEBTS

The problem: *Kerrie and Jack live with their two daughters, Sally, nine, and Penny, seven, in a three-bedroom brick veneer home which they rent for $420 a fortnight. In the past ten years, this couple has had practically every kind of financial setback known to man; including severe ill-health, retrenchment and accidents, and they have been seriously ripped off more than once.*

They work as hard as their health permits. Jack works as a cleaner and mows extra lawns, while Kerrie relies on family payments and her hobby making greeting cards. But with credit cards now maxed out and some bills still unpaid, a car loan and fortnightly expenses running at $1210.00, they are slipping deeper into the money pit at the rate of $30 to $120 every *pay. They need a new washing machine and would like to afford insurance for their belongings, but ongoing medical costs have robbed their savings and their hopes.*

The solution: At current interest rates and only $50 repayments a fortnight, it will take Kerrie and Jack more than four years to repay their $4000 credit card debt. But they can solve their financial problems in about six to 12 months—depending on how hard they try—just by finding little savings everywhere to make extra repayments, and by adopting my radical new approach to credit cards—as explained in chapter 8: How to House-train your Credit Card.

Radical credit card attack: By using Trick 1 from chapter 8 to pay their entire income (minus wallet money) straight into their credit card and leaving it sit there until needed, this couple can save $48 a month—and that's not even counting EFTPOS or bank account fees which they don't need to pay anymore by doing this. Also, with only one card in the family, Jack will have to be with Kerrie every time she shops—and you know how much men love shopping!

They can also use Trick 2 paying credit with credit. (Once only!) This is because their current CBA Bankcard has a reasonable interest rate of only 14.3% with no annual fee, but charges interest straight away on purchases. A CBA Mastercard, however, with a 55-day free interest rate, has a 2% higher interest, and a $45 annual fee, but has a loyalty scheme with a host of freebies. Sounds more expensive, but in this case, it's not.

If their application is approved, they can use their Mastercard to pay out their Bankcard—paying credit with credit. Do it before they deposit their first pay, and the balance will be over $3600, so they'll earn enough loyalty points—called True Awards points—to get their first annual fee refunded, or get a voucher for up to $50 off a washing machine from David Jones!

Yes, they might have up to $80 a year extra to pay because of the higher interest rate, but only if they slack off on their budget and their Mastercard remains full the whole time.

They'll get a 55-day free period, however, when they get the new card, which will save them $86 in one hit!

Tricks 3 and 4 from chapter 8 can also provide advantages in the form of free—and much-needed—shopping vouchers through the awards scheme attached to their new credit card. In this couple's case, their spending could earn them between $100 and $300 worth of vouchers a year at useful places like Caltex, David Jones and Video Ezy, not to mention a wide range of holiday specials, so our couple really can get something for nothing.

Housekeeping: Most single income families with one to four children seem to spend between $120 and $280 a fortnight. Because of her health, however, Kerrie spends a lot more—because she finds cooking very difficult and often relies on pre-cooked, semi-prepared or takeaway meals to save her sanity. But by cooking bigger meals once or twice a week, and freezing the extras for next week, she can still enjoy the luxury of not having to cook some nights and save $50 to $80 a fortnight in the process.

Prescriptions: Kerrie still has a little way to go before she has spent over $631.20 in the one year—enough to qualify her for cheaper scripts under Centrelink's CN card. But because their combined income is $550 a week or less, they can apply for a Low Income Health Card—also through Centrelink—which does allow Kerrie to qualify for the $3.30 scripts and saves her *$45 a month* from now on. (She'll have her new washing machine before Christmas!)

Books: Kerrie loves reading and can save an average of *$6 a pay* by joining her town library instead of buying books that she might not read again.

McDonald's meals: Kerrie suffers chronic depression, so a meal out two or three times a week is a much-needed break from the kitchen as well as a reward for the children for helping her around the house. At present the family orders two quarter pounder meal'n'drink deals for $5.95 each, plus two small chips, two small drinks and nine chicken nuggets for the girls to share for $9.60, totalling $20.50 per visit. But if they do what we do, they can get four Happy Meals—a drink, small chips and burger, any of which can be upgraded for a few cents extra—all for only $14.20, *saving $6.30 per visit.* That's cheaper than the equivalent of four McDonald's visits for the old price of three. And there's the added bonus of collecting all happy-meal toys faster than any other two-child family in town!

More importantly, at two McDonald's visits a month, they'll save more than enough to pay for up to $35,000-worth of contents insurance through most insurance companies!

Church dinners: They like to buy hot Sunday dinners at their church every week, but cutting down to only once a fortnight instead of twice, they can save *$32 a month.* (Yes, by the way, GST does apply to meals sold at church.) An even cheaper alternative would be to join a bowls or other club and eat out before socialising at church.

Children's school banking: $2 a fortnight banked for each girl will be flat out earning the kids 50 cents a year in interest. Instead, put that money into your credit card ready to buy uniforms and books, and you'll *save up to $17 a year* in interest!

Current cash: At the moment, they can scrape up about $100 in savings, so if they close their savings accounts, and put the money off their credit card, they'll save $9 a month on bank fees and $16 interest off their credit card over the next 12 months. Don't think of it as spending that money, leaving them no savings to fall back on. Think of it as parking their savings in their credit card until they can pay it off.

Phone: Assuming she makes more than 50 calls a month, Kerrie can save an average of $4 a month by upgrading her Telstra line rental from $17.50 to $19.50 a month—which sounds backwards, but it drops her 22-cent phone calls down to 18.50-cent phone calls and still entitles her to the new 15-cent neighbourhood rates. Also, while she can't ditch the phone for health reasons, she might be eligible for an extra 5% discount, by switching mobile phone companies and combining her mobile and home phone accounts onto one bill.

Disability Support Pension: In addition to the Low Income Health Card, Kerrie can ask for an application for Disability Support Pension from Centrelink, which she needs to discuss with her doctor. If her GP agrees that her health makes her unfit for work, then her doctor will supply a Treating Doctor's Report to attach to her application. Based on this family's income, Kerrie could be entitled to a support pension of up to $135.00 a fortnight.

Tax deduction: If total medical expenses for the financial year exceed $1000—including any prescriptions or hospital, dental or doctor fees etc.—then Jack will be entitled to an additional tax deduction. See Tax Pack under Net Medical Expenses for more details.

CASE STUDY 5: UNPREDICTABLE INCOMES (SELF-EMPLOYED)

The problem: *Tammy and Daniel live with their daughters Kirra-Lee, aged four, and Jayden, aged two, in a new three-bedroom brick home, which they built 18 months ago near Adelaide, SA. While Tammy stays home to care for their children, Daniel sub-contracts as a carpenter building homes. He works long hours, but his income was less than $16,000 last year after a builder went bankrupt without paying him. He was unable to get Centrelink assistance because he was self-employed. The couple was struck again by bad luck when their only car—Daniel's sole transport to jobs—blew its motor, costing them thousands to repair. Their biggest problem is not knowing when they will get their next payment.*

Goal 1: To organise their finances to survive between contract payments.

Goal 2: To replace the rotting chipboard on their make-shift kitchen bench with a new benchtop, expected cost: $1000.

The solution: This young family is in severe financial distress. They never know when—or if—their next payment will arrive. They have zero cash reserves. And including their credit card, which is now full, they have four loans; not to mention debts to friends, relatives and local businesses. They've already been forced to trim all the extras from their budget. But they can save thousands and make life much easier on their pockets by completely re-organising the way their finances are structured.

Loan amalgamation: Tammy and Daniel have debts totalling nearly $124,000 on interest rates ranging from 7.7% to 27% and their repayments total a whopping $700 a fortnight! But their home is worth $170,000, and they only owe $114,000, which means they have equity in their home to the value of $56,000.

Tammy and Daniel can use this equity to refinance all of their loans onto one big loan with a cheaper interest rate and a more manageable repayment. Increase the loan to a grand total of $124,000, and they can also achieve their goal of being able to afford to finish their kitchen by replacing the rotting chipboard with a new hygienic benchtop.

Most banks these days offer mortgage offset accounts. But with the help of free national mortgage broker Mortgage Choice—who organised all the paperwork and valuations—we chose the ANZ All-In-One Account for this particular couple, because it has no fees on the loan or on the account. At the time it had a honeymoon interest rate of 6.9%, going up to the fairly common variable rate of 7.8% in the second year. The loan also has a credit card facility to help them pay bills until their next contract payment arrives. And it encourages them to keep at least $2000 aside for emergencies, with the added bonus of being able to draw back any extra repayments on the loan in a few years, when it's time to replace that ageing work vehicle (if they haven't been able to save up for it in the meantime).

Total repayments per fortnight are now $430, an immediate saving of $270/fn!

These savings should be used to repay business accounts, friends and family, in that order. Then with the money they put aside for paying bills, this couple should be able to scrape up that minimum $2000 for emergencies in just a few months, making sure they get the best benefits out of their mortgage offset account too. They'll still have to budget strictly for the next few months, but at least now they should be able to cope a lot easier with long waits between Daniel's payments.

Warning: Their car loan, car repairs, existing credit card and kitchen benchtop loans are NOT gone. They are cheaper per fortnight because they are combined with the home loan at a cheaper interest rate, and the fact they are now being paid out over 30 years, instead of two or three. Tammy and Daniel no longer *have* to pay $700 a fortnight in repayments, but for those fortnights when they can afford it, I strongly recommend that they do. It will swipe up to 17 years off their loan!

Budgeting: Most people work out their budgets by seeing how much they earn, then deciding how best to spend it. Strict budgeters, however, and **people with unpredictable incomes** like Tammy and Daniel, **need to work their budgets out backwards:** when you get paid, figure out the minimum amount you need to survive each week—including savings for your next bills. Add as much as you can—two to four weeks worth of groceries if possible—as a safety margin. Then leave it sitting in your mortgage offset account until needed (again, saving stacks on home loan interest). Then if there's anything left over from your pay, use it to build up a bigger safety net for those little home improvements you're working towards, a small holiday to save your sanity, or perhaps a work ute to replace your car and trailer (also making rego and insurance cheaper).

Bill savings: This couple needs to start saving for their bills in advance. They should put their savings in the mortgage offset account, and once they've saved $2000 they'll also save $2500 in interest over the term of the loan.

Car repairs: Next time, instead of refinancing or putting big car repairs on credit, this couple should ask their mechanic about negotiating a repayment scheme with between 5% and 10% a year interest. That's cheaper for them, but still an incentive for him or her to agree, because it's more money for the mechanic in the long run.

Tax deduction: Their car's motor blowing up was bad luck. But blowing up when they were using it for business, and waiting to blow up until this financial year instead of last financial year—when they got all their tax back anyway—was very good luck. That's because the cost of repairs, the cost of getting a loan to pay for them, and the interest on the loan are all tax deductible. Also, if they refinance this loan with their home loan as suggested, then they can count a percentage of the home loan interest as tax deductible too. (Refinancing fees would also have been partially tax deductible, but this loan didn't have any.)

Did you know

A prominent Australian reporter recently complained to me that no matter how hard she tried, she kept losing track of her budget after a few pays, so she kept spending her savings by accident.

Her problem was her mortgage offset account. Her entire income went into her offset savings account, where it stayed while she bought everything on credit card or EFTPOS. But after bank fees and purchases were deducted, she could never tell how much was left in her bank account for bills, Christmas savings and her nest-egg.

As a busy professional, it all got too much for her too quickly. She'd give up in disgust and let her everyday spending gobble it away.

'Simple,' I said. 'Just transfer your monthly savings for these things automatically into a savings account or term deposit. That way, you can't spend it by accident.'

She was horrified. 'But it's a mortgage offset account! I need the money in there to reduce the interest I pay on my home loan!'

'Look,' I said, 'how much do you usually keep aside for bills?'

'About two grand,' she said. 'Sometimes a little more,

but bills usually wipe it out completely about twice a year and it takes a while to build up again.'

'Great,' I said. 'Your home loan interest is 8%, so you're keeping two grand in your offset account to save you a max of $160 a year. Meanwhile, your budget keeps blowing out because you can't keep track of it, and you're accidentally over-spending about six grand a year in savings.'

After I picked her jaw up off the ground, she hurried off to her bank to make the changes. Remember: like everything else, you should use your bank accounts to suit YOUR lifestyle, not a bank brochure.

18

L-plate Investing

Okay, so you've got your financial life on track, you're starting to feel secure and it's time to consider building your assets. You need to know about investment options.

THE GIST OF IT
Practically anyone can build a healthy investment portfolio and supplement their regular income without having to work up a sweat. And yes, it is relatively simple; but more importantly, it's fun.

You don't have to be overly smart, talented, lucky or greedy. You just need a little faith and a bit more patience. It's called investing in the stockmarket—and I mean *investing*. I'm not talking about day-trading, options, futures or borrowing money to negative-gear shares—you can try any of those once your nerves are a little more metallic.

Get started by having a trial run—two to six months as a 'virtual' investor with no money outlay whatsoever to see if you've got the nerves for staying sane as a long-term shareholder. Then—and only then—use my checklist, hints and tips to accumulate a decent investment portfolio at your own pace.

Are you crazy!? I hear some of you scream. *Suggesting that school-leavers and low-income earners should bet on shares?* Hmmm...

maybe, but it's not actually betting. It relies on research and a long-term view. And while it's not by any means guaranteed, if you do it the smart way, the probability is very high that you will come out substantially ahead (most times between 20% and 60%).

Before I go any further, I do need to stress—LOUDLY—a handful of very important facts:

1. Everything I learned—everything I'm about to explain—I had to learn the hard way. I don't have any formal qualifications in stock analysis, but this is the method I used to accumulate nearly $60,000 in my first 18 months of investing when I had—on average—only a dozen companies in the portfolio. And yes, there were always one or two slower performers, but that's to be expected. I didn't need to get paranoid over watching the market every day and since it's fun and easy, it's the method I still use today.

2. There are no secrets here. All the information comes from investor brochures, from library books, my stockbroker and the Australian Stock Exchange (ASX). The only difference is that this is the easy-to-understand, plain English version!

Did you know?

By the end of 1999, after Telstra, Commonwealth Bank, TAB and a few major insurance companies had listed on the stock exchange, a whopping 40% of the Australian adult population had become shareholders. Many insurance policy holders—people who had never owned shares before—were issued with them practically automatically.

This created a renewed effort to make prospectus details easier to read for L-plate investors. But ongoing support has been available only to those who seek it.

Like children handed a sealed box of Lego, many low-income and ageing people were given a great opportunity, without the knowledge to access the goodies inside or the skills to build something bigger and better.

3. There are many ways to choose shares and every investor enjoys their own quirks as to how and why they buy or sell—these steps are the gist of most methods. Adopt and adapt them to suit yourself when you're ready.

4. You don't lose money on shares, unless you SELL them for less than you paid for them. If the price of your shares falls for whatever reason, don't panic. You haven't lost money YET, because if your company is a good company with a good product, performs strongly against its competitors and is still paying a good dividend, the price will go up again in the future. Why sell it for a loss now, just because someone has put a scare into the market? (Unless you're going to be sneaky and offset a capital loss against a capital gain for the financial year, which I'll get to in a sec.)

> **Beginners should invest only in good companies with good customer service, good products and good market placing.**

NOT JUST FOR THE RICH AND GREEDY

You don't have to be rich or greedy to invest in shares. There's no assets test to get you in the door, although brokers may ask you to fill in details of your assets. But this isn't to make you feel like you're out of your league. It's to get an idea of what gaps they can suggest need filling in your investment portfolio.

NO NEED TO QUIBBLE OVER PRICES

If you're going to quibble or panic over one or two cents' difference in share price when it's time to buy or sell, then you need to ask someone to whack you over the head with a reality stick. Even on a reasonably sized parcel of about 10,000 shares, you're really only worrying about $200 when you're actually pocketing thousands more in the longer run.

When you're used to bare-backside-budgeting, it can be

hard not to focus on this 'extra' $200, I know. But if you're a beginner on the stockmarket, then you'd better learn to relax or you won't last long and you have to last, because it's in the long term that the safest money lies.

START WITH NOTHING

By using a portion of your long-term savings, you can use the information in this chapter to buy a small part of a strong viable company or various companies (up to 20 of them eventually from as many different industries as you can) in order to broaden your investment portfolio.

NO LOYALTY REQUIRED

You don't have to be loyal to shares. You can own stakes in fierce competitors if you like, like Coles and Woolworths or Westpac and National Bank. Then sit back and watch the competition with a cheeky grin, because you're in a win-win box seat.

DIFFERENT STRATEGIES FOR DIFFERENT REASONS

As I've mentioned, there are different ways to invest, depending on what you need your shares portfolio to do for you. A widow soon to retire for example, might invest her husband's life insurance payout into low-yield blue chip shares to produce a predictable supplement income which places little risk on the principal and still allows her to receive a pension. But a super-charged 30-year-old who likes tax benefits and negative-gearing might prefer to chase big capital gains, regardless of the dividend income.

My preferred option is a cautious combination. This method seeks both regular income and long-term growth and achieves it by investing in ordinary shares from a broad range of companies to sit on for three to five years. Yes, you *can* cash particularly good gains when they occur and then re-invest it in other areas, the idea being to spread and reduce your investment risk without needing to be greedy or paranoid.

When you buy, you'll be buying when stocks are under-valued based on sound, simple analysis of their finances and performances, which I'll teach you.

When you sell at higher prices you'll use the same theories. And when you take your gains, have no regrets if the price goes higher after you've sold. It's your portfolio that matters, after all, not those of investors who are gamer to place their necks on the chopping block. You don't have to wait for prices to hit bottom or peak when you buy or sell. Just buying lowish and selling highish is enough to make your investments swell. Before you invest in *anything* you should understand how things work, so before I get to the ten steps, here's a very basic guide to things you need to know. (See also Shares Jargon in the Appendix.)

> **Buy lowish, sell highish, no regrets.**

WHAT ELSE TRADES ON THE STOCKMARKET?

Ordinary shares are the most commonly traded security on the stockmarket, because they're easy to accumulate and manage. Ordinary shares are called **equity securities**, because they raise money by granting partial ownership in a company or in a special project (like a toll road). Other kinds of equity securities that you will come across as a beginner include *bonus issues*, *rights issues*, and *company options*, which are designed to encourage existing shareholders to invest even more, often for a specific reason (eg. modernising an existing factory). Then there's **preference shares**, which are much like ordinary shares, except they're dearer to buy because they usually pay bigger dividends and if the company goes bankrupt, preference shares get paid out before ordinary shares do.

More complicated equity securities include **listed property trusts, listed equity trusts, financial futures** and **exchange traded options,** which I won't go into in this book.

Debt securities are also traded on the ASX as a way for organisations to borrow money from investors, instead of from banks and other lenders. They're called **bonds** if you get them from a government or semi-government body, or **debentures**, if you get them from listed companies and they're all generally safe and easy for L-plate investors to buy; however, returns are usually lower in exchange for lower risk.

Convertible notes are a hybrid—a combination of debt and equity securities.

Managed funds and other investment schemes: As well as investing directly in shares, you can also get into the market by making regular payments into investment schemes. Many financial institutions now give you the opportunity to invest seductively affordable monthly amounts into mixed parcels of shares, with the promise that your 'mixed basket' will consist of the finest fruit: usually investing in just the blue chip shares.

For people without the knowledge or the initial $2000 you need to get started on your own, these schemes can seem reasonable. Risk is spread over a basket of mixed shares instead of sinking your entire small investment into one company. This is also sound investment theory. But there are also problems.

First, many of these schemes have hefty administration fees. Second, some of these schemes are not investments in the actual shares of the companies, but are in what is called leveraged securities on those shares (like warrants or futures) which introduces a whole new level of assumptions into the forecasts for returns. All reputable schemes explain these assumptions in their prospectus or brochures, and you should always seek to understand the implications of these assumptions BEFORE you sign up for your investment. If you're just starting out, it really can be easier to invest in shares directly by yourself.

Warning: Always double-check investment forecasts for yourself.

> ### . What if I don't have $2000?
>
> Then don't spend that much. You could buy as little as $100 worth of shares in a company if you were that way inclined, it's just that you'll still be paying the (usual) minimum $50 brokerage fees whether you spend $200 or $2000.

Note: Investment schemes often advertise returns over 15 to 30 years, but beware: you can lose serious money if you have to get out in under ten years or so. Double-check short-term forecasts (as well as long-term forecasts) for yourself!!!

One 'reputable' investment scheme I investigated recently bragged that my initial $300,000 would grow to $620,000 over 20 years. They neglected to tell me that my 'investment' would be worth $13,647.00 LESS after one year, getting worse year after year until after ten years it would be worth $111,667 LESS than what I had kicked off with. Only after that did it start to improve, due only to the way the investment was structured. By comparison, you can expect at least one of your 20 companies to double in value inside almost any three-year period. (Usually you can do heaps better than that!)

CONTROL VS. MANAGEMENT

To invest in any managed fund also means giving up full control of your investment. Most people don't have a problem with that because the people you're entrusting with your money are usually experienced professionals. But I do have a problem surrendering control, because of the number of times I—and friends and family—have been let down by 'investment experts'.

Also—and more interestingly—most of the L-plate investors I know have a similar success/error rate to some of the big investment houses. The difference is, we have the pleasure of being able to do something about our mistakes by learning from them instead of feeling helpless if the investment manager consistently under-performs.

> **It's your money. You worked hard for it. Why let someone else have all the fun playing with it?**

SHARES: THE OTHER BENEFITS

Aside from the money they can make you when you buy low and sell high, shares have many other benefits, including dividends and re-investment plans, franking, capital gain/loss offsetting, shareholder discounts, tax deductible holidays, no annual or ongoing fees—and a new ego for you. Here's what I mean:

DIVIDENDS

Twice a year most companies pay dividends to everyone who owns their shares on their 'books closing date'. Dates are advertised in financial newspapers ahead of time, so buying shares in a company which is about to pay its dividend *can* sometimes earn you a quick cash sweetener without having to sell the share—as long as you're not paying for it by having to buy the share at a higher than usual price because everyone else is trying to do the same thing.

FRANKING

The majority of companies on the stockmarket issue shares which are fully franked. To oversimplify, this means that company tax has already been paid on the shares, and the Tax Office therefore considers that you have already paid 34% tax (class 'c' company tax rate, for example) on any dividends you get paid from these shares.

So if your personal tax rate is zero (because you don't work) then you will get the full 34% back when you put in your tax return. If your personal tax rate is the more common 30% (for people who earn $20,001 to $50,000), then you'll get 4% back —which is HEAPS better than term deposits (or shares that are un-franked), because you have to fork out tax for these at the end of the year at your top tax rate.

To make you go 'wow', consider this: 600 shares which
have a dividend yield of 5% and pay a fully franked
dividend of 15 cents will pay you $90.00 AND send
$46.36 to the Tax Office on your behalf as a franking
credit (also called an imputation credit). But a term
deposit which pays you 5% interest will pay you $90, out
of which you'll have to pay $27 in tax.

DIVIDEND RE-INVESTMENT PLANS (DRPs)

These are optional re-investment schemes offered by some
companies which permit you to get your dividend paid to you
as more shares instead of cash. The new shares are often given
to you at a discount and are always transferred to you without
brokerage fees, making them a real bargain. DRPs help your
investment grow faster, because next time your dividend is
calculated, it's calculated on a higher number of shares—much
like compounding interest.

CAPITAL LOSS/GAIN OFFSETTING

Shares can help you to legitimately minimise your tax.

If—for example –you sell one parcel of *Rocket Inc* shares to
get a profit of $2000, you have to pay tax on this capital gain.
BUT, if you also happen to have a parcel of *Yoyo Inc* shares that
are worth about $2000 less than what you paid for them, you
can sell these shares to create a 'paper loss' of $2000. You can
then buy your *Yoyo* shares back at the lower price (even the
same day if you wish). You now have a $2000 loss to offset
against your $2000 gain, so overall you don't pay any tax, *and*
you still have your *Yoyo Inc* shares for when the price goes back
up again. You just have to be careful next time you sell *Yoyo Inc*
so you minimise tax on the much higher capital gain on them
next time round.

SHAREHOLDER DISCOUNTS

Some companies offer discounts and other benefits to their
shareholders.

Here's a few examples which were current at time of publication.

Note: Minimum share purchases may be required.

Company	Details of discounts offered
Amalgamated Holdings	10% off ski, ski school, and ski clothing at NSW's Thredbo Alpine Village, plus discounts to other hotels and resorts in the group and BC&C and Greater Union cinema discounts.
ANZ Bank	Discounts or exemptions on assorted bank fees, $100 discount on loan applications, 20% off home insurance, 26.5% off life & travel insurance, 1% off personal loan fixed rates, and bonus 0.25% interest on savings.
Ariadne Ltd	Voucher booklet for $50 of casual parking at Kings Carparks.
Blackmores	25% off Blackmores and VitaGlow products purchased directly from the company.
Club Crocodile	$50 off standard room rates at Cairns & Whitsundays resorts, plus $50 off one lunch for two a year on Kookaburra Queen paddlewheeler, 5 free nights for two per year at Long Island Resort.
Coles Myer	10% off general merchandise and 5% off furniture, whitegoods, audio and computer equipment at Myer/Grace Bros; 5% off purchases at Coles, Red Rooster, Liquorland, Pick'n'pay and Officeworks; 3% off at BiLo and Newmart; 7.5% off at Fossey's, Kmart, World4Kids and Target; and 10% off at Katies.
Jupiters Ltd	10% off meals, merchandise and entertainment at Conrad Jupiters Brisbane and the Gold Coast, plus special offers on stage productions.
Brian McGuigan Wines	10% off wines plus special offers.
OPSM	Voucher sent with annual report for 10% off OPSM and Protector Safety products.
Pacific Dunlop	5% discount on goods supplied by Goodyear Auto Service, Marshall Batteries, Lawrence & Hanson, Repco Auto Parts, Electrical Depot Beaurepaires for tyres and Dunlop Super Dealers.
Palmer Corporation	20% off Jag purchases.
PMP Communications	25% off *TV Week*, *TV Hits*, *New Idea*, *Home Beautiful*, *Your Garden* and *Girlfriend* subscriptions.
Village Roadshow	12 vouchers a year of 'buy one get one free' per year for Birch, Carroll and Coyle, Village, Greater Union and Palace Cinemas.

| Walker Corporation | 5% off the purchase price of any of the company's medium density residential development units. |
| Westpac Bank | $500 off loan establishment fees for some loans, bonus interest rates on some term deposits, and no monthly fees on various current accounts. |

TAX DEDUCTIBLE HOLIDAYS (TO ATTEND AGMs)

Tax perks for your average blue-collar worker are next to non-existent. But as a shareholder, just about anyone with a reasonable investment (see your accountant for details) can justify at least one trip interstate or overseas a year to attend the annual general meeting of a company in which you're a shareholder.

Don't pick your stocks just because they hold their AGM in Vanuatu or Tahiti and don't think you can buy a few shares in two or three companies just to get two or three tax deductible holidays a year. The Tax Office is watching you. You can't claim ticket entries into theme parks for the family while you're in town. But you can claim petrol to and from home to the venue where the AGM is and to and from the venue and your hotel as well as meals and accommodation for each shareholder. If you stay longer or do other things with your family while you're in the area, it's at your private expense.

NO ANNUAL FEES

Unlike most savings accounts, share ownership costs you *nothing* in annual fees or charges. But there will be a brokerage fee on all your transactions.

A NEW EGO

Look forward to a morale boost if you buy shares. You not only own a portion of the company, but all the stock on its shelves, its trucks that overtake you on the highway, and the land (and carparks) it owns in every town. Hundreds of stores, thousands of employees, and countless support companies, all working like busy little bees—and all for us (shareholders). Makes you feel good to be alive, or at least, that's how I choose to think about it.

MORE REASONS WHY SHARES ARE BETTER THAN BANK ACCOUNTS FOR LONG-TERM INVESTMENTS

- Shares pay dividends—which is similar to bank interest—but your principal investment in shares also grows in value. Money in bank accounts, however, is only worth what you put in, plus interest (minus fees).
- Shares allow you to choose the level of risk and return that suits you, but you have to take what you're given with bank accounts.
- 'Franking' on dividends means that tax is paid for you on your dividends, so it's possible to get a tax refund—unlike bank interest, on which you pay tax.
- It only takes about three days to get your money when you sell shares. Term deposits can take longer if you don't want to get slugged with penalties.
- If you time it right, you only have to own shares for a few days to get six months worth of dividends; but you have to have money in term deposits for the full term to get a similar return.
- You can offset capital losses against capital gains on sales of shares, but you can't offset anything against bank interest.
- You're entitled to a tax deduction for travel, accommodation and attendance at your company's annual general meeting. But you get nothing for going to an ATM, except maybe robbed every now and again.
- Shares give you a regular opportunity once every year to vote out any directors who aren't managing your investments to your satisfaction; but you may have to put up with your bank manager until he or she retires.

WHERE TO GET THE SKINNY ON SHARES

There are stacks of places to research the latest gossip cheaply on shares and companies in which to invest, including: invest-ment magazines, the ASX website at www.asx.com.au, the 'Small Business Show' and 'Business Sunday' on the Nine

Network every Sunday morning, and your personal stockbroker and their monthly newsletter.

Nothing beats the hands-on experience of people who are in the market every working minute. Brokerage costs start at 2.5% of your trade for the two-legged human variety, often with a minimum of $50 (which is why a starting investment of $2000 is recommended: 2.5% of 2000 = $50. Yes, you can start with less, it just means you fall a fly-wing short of getting the best value for your $50.). Online brokers are about half that price, but that's because there's no personal service or advice. Although their industry and company reports are often available on their websites, online brokers also usually restrict you to buying or selling 'at market'—which means they don't hold your orders to get you the best deal. *And* they can't give you a second opinion on your shortlist, and if you're an L-plate budgeter, you might need that to make it through step 8.

The most accessible, cheap, reliable and informative resource is the *Australian Financial Review*, a newspaper published six days a week with extensive market reports, company announcements, easy-to-read statistic summaries, and an index on the back page which shows you at a glance which companies are mentioned in that issue. It costs approx. $2.50 per issue and this will be tax deductible when you own shares.

QUESTIONS TO ASK YOURSELF BEFORE INVESTING

Before you invest money anywhere—even into term deposits—you should know what you want from your investment. For example, do you want a safe place to stick your nest-egg that won't devour it with fees and will give you a modest amount of interest into the bargain? Then you want a term deposit.

If you are prepared for more risk and more rewards, then you should consider the stockmarket.

This chapter hopes to open your eyes to the possibilities of what you can do with the savings that you find in every other chapter.

Important: Ask yourself the following questions to evaluate what kind of investor you are. The middle column shows you my answers on your behalf, so you have an idea of what the ten steps we'll get to soon are aiming at achieving for you.

Ask yourself	Me sticking words in your gob for now	Your actual answer
Do you wish to invest money?	Yeah, cool. Why not?	
Do you have money to invest that you don't need in the short-term and might otherwise stick in a long-term deposit?	I do now that I've worked through the earlier chapters.	
Are you investing for security?	You bet.	
Are you investing for income? (Investors chasing income usually go for preference shares which are dearer, but often have guaranteed higher dividends.)	Yeah, but I still have yonks to retirement, so it's not as important.	
Are you investing for capital gain?	Well, that's where the money is, isn't it?	
What rate of return are you seeking?	Anything better than bank interest is great, but I'll shoot for 10–15% after tax and fees. That's keen, but not too greedy.	
What do you want to achieve from the investment?	To beat inflation, get in on the shareholder benefits and re-invest any gains, so I just keep getting richer.	
Over what period do you want to invest?	Not sure . . . 5 to 15 years?	
What risks are you prepared to take?	Bugger all.	
How big an investment are you aiming to put in during the short term?	$2000 to $20,000 in the first year I reckon.	
Do you earn taxable income from a job etc.?	Yep, I'm a low-paid slave all right.	

If your answers are not similar to the ones I've suggested, then there's little point reading on as this method is not for you. But if you do proceed, ask yourself these questions again in about a year to help you keep on target with your portfolio.

WHAT YOU'RE AIMING TO DO

A small portion of slower achievers (or under-achievers) in a portfolio is normal. Get used to the idea. Then ensure the overall success of your portfolio by purchasing small share parcels in 12 to 20 companies across all types of industries from banking, tourism and retail, to manufacturing, mining and medical. You're aiming for a balanced portfolio.

CREATING A SHORTLIST TO BUY

First step is get today's issue of the *Financial Review* and run your ruler down the list of every ordinary share that's listed on the stock exchange, noting the details of any that satisfy the needs of each of the following ten steps into a shortlist of 'cautious potentials'.

Shortlisting shares should take you about one cup of coffee, two Tim Tams, and $2500 to spend per share parcel including fees.

When the sharemarket is generally sluggish, your shortlist is likely to be quite long—as many as 20—because buyers are scarce, share prices fall and bargains appear. However, when the market is charging along, prices rise and bargains become less common. You might only have six or so potential companies on your shortlist. Don't let either situation worry you. As an L-plate investor, you're only looking for ONE company to buy at a time.

Compare companies on your shortlist a few times, getting fussier each time, until you have three to five companies to investigate thoroughly at step 8. A few inquiries later at step 9 and you should have two or three good companies to choose from for step 10.

You can sell as many shares as you own however you choose, but you can only buy them rounded to the nearest 100.

Handy hint: Budget an extra $300–$500 for roughly each $2000-worth of shares. Brokerage fees, stamp duty and GST on brokerage total only around $60 but you'll need the extra for rounding up or down to the nearest marketable parcel.

YOUR CRASH COURSE

The table is your crash course in reading stockmarket reports.
No trembling—it's not that scary.

LAST MINUTE THINGS YOU NEED TO KNOW
See also Shares Jargon on page 258

THE P/E RATIO (P/E = PRICE TO EARNINGS RATIO)
P/E ratios under 6 usually indicate the share is due for a bounce-back. Companies with much smaller P/E ratios can be great value but tend to take longer to recover.

P/E ratios between 14 and 18 are starting to get overpriced. (*Note:* Many good companies, especially blue chips, trade at P/E ratios higher than 14. That's because volume of sales based on popularity keep the prices inflated—until they hit hard times, of course, when they shrivel up like any other stock.)

P/E ratio = share price ÷ earnings per share

Warning: This is a historical statistic. It's calculated on the last dividend and assumes the dividend will be the same again next time. Obviously, this assumption is not entirely reliable. Struggling companies may have to reduce or cancel their next dividend, while thriving companies may announce bigger dividends. But even with this flawed assumption, the P/E ratio is a useful tool for refining your shortlist of 'cautious potentials'.

All companies react differently to market and economic forces, but generally:

A low P/E ratio in comparison to the P/E ratios of that company's competitors or of companies operating in similar fields, indicates that the sharemarket expects that company to perform a little slower than the others.

(Lower P/E = poorer performance.)

A higher P/E ratio for that company over similar companies can mean either:

- the market expects it to perform better, or
- the company is being valued for its asset backing, not for its earnings potential.

As a rule of thumb—for cautious investors—try looking for companies with a P/E ratio between 6 and 14.

Because companies usually report their earnings about the end of the financial year, P/E ratios are the most reliable between July and December each year.

If the share price falls after you buy: it's annoying— a little worrying perhaps—but remind yourself that all companies go through cycles. Well-managed companies with strong dividend yields and good product will nearly always see a strong performance in the medium to long term.

So how do you do it? How do you pick which shares are a good buy? Read on. It's actually not that hard.

Industrial markets (includes all companies that are not primarily mining or oil companies)

52-week High	Low	Company name	Mrkt call code	Last sale	+ or −	Vol 100s	Quotes Buy Sell	Div'd c per share	NTA	Div yld %	P/E ratio
This column is for the highest price paid within last 52 weeks in $s.	Lowest price paid within last 52 weeks in $s. (Some market reports have a column for highs and lows for the day, not the year.)	Abbreviated name of company. (Industrial stocks often have an ASX code column beside this one with a code for searching the ASX website for daily market results)	4 digit code for checking latest share prices by phone. Call 1902 941 520 and enter codes for the shares you want to check. Warning: Costs start at $1 a minute.	Last price paid before close of market that day in $s.	Shows difference between last price of shares that day and the day before in cents.	Total number of shares traded that day in thousands.	How much people were offering to buy or sell the shares for in $s, just before the market closed for the day.	How many cents per share was paid as the last dividend. (This column also shows franking codes.)	Net tangible assets, shown in $s per share.	Dividend calculated as a % of the last sale price.	Price earnings ratio.

Note: The 'Company name' column may also include special codes, including: rts = rights issue   new = new shares opt = options, (which sometimes include a date they're due)   pf = preference shares   conv pref = convertible preferences cn = convertible notes

There are others, but these are the main ones and once you get the hang of them, you can usually work out the codes by yourself.

TEN SPEEDY STEPS TO BUYING SHARES

Instructions: Turn to the market reports in the back of today's *Australian Financial Review*—or any other detailed daily market reports. Follow these steps and fill out the table on the next page with your 'cautious potentials' from both the industrial AND resource market reports.

Slide your ruler down the dividend yield column looking for companies in your range, and when you find one fill in your table with the details of the companies that interest you.

- If it's a company with a dubious reputation, lousy product or customer service, pass it by.
- If it's a company you recognise as reputable AND if its current share price is at least 8% higher than its 52-week low AND if it still has 30% or more to rise to reach its 52-week high, then add it to your list of cautious potentials.

(*Note*: These figures are flexible. As your confidence grows, flex the limits to suit yourself: 8% up from the low is usually an indication that the share price has bottomed out and could be heading up again, 30% or more below the high gives an encouraging indication of how much your investment will grow next time the price peaks. Since share prices peak or bottom out for a billion different reasons, you'll ask your stockbroker later why each company on your list has experienced its annual high and low. If there's not much difference between highs and lows, the company is fairly stable at those values.)

- If it's a company you don't recognise, you can still add it to your shortlist IF it satisfies the above rule, but you'll have to research it more thoroughly at step 8.

That's the gist of it. Now it's time for some serious money fun!

STEP 1: LEARNING WITH VIRTUAL STOCKS

Play with virtual shares until you get the hang of things by reading market reports at least three times a week for at least a month. Select between five and 20 'virtual stocks'—stocks that you might have bought IF you had the money. Then keep an eye on them—not only for the rest of your trial month, but for as many months as you find it fun to do so.

STEP 2: START YOUR SHORTLIST

a) Kick off your shortlist table (like the example below) with companies whose shareholder discounts interest you. If your stockbroker has recommended companies, add these now to compare later.

b) Add any blue chip companies—top 150 market leaders which are usually published in their own table at the top of most market reports—that are at or near their 52-week low.

mpany	Div %	Franking code	$ Last Sale	52 wk high	52 week low	P/E	EPS	What do they do	Shareholder discount?	Gearing ratio
Caltex	11	f	2.29	3.3	1.75	5.7	40	Fuel—(everyone needs it)	No	See step 8

STEP 3: A DECENT FRANKED DIVIDEND AND SHARE PRICE

Run your finger down the dividend yield column of your market report. In the industrial stocks look for dividends between 7% and 12%. For resource stocks, look between 4% and 7%. When you find one, use your ruler to read across the correct company name that belongs to that dividend yield.

If it's a company you personally wouldn't deal with unless tortured, pass it by. Otherwise, check the entry in the dividend cents/share column to see what the franking code is. No code = no franking, p = partly franked, f = fully franked.

You're looking for dividends with an 'f' code, because their real value is at around 3% higher than the equivalent bank interest because tax has been pre-paid for you at company tax rates. If you find one, go to step 4 before adding it to your list.

Notes: The ranges 7%–12%, and 4%–7% are personal choices at a time when interest on term deposits is between 3% and 6%. You can see the pattern and yes, there are plenty of good companies with yields outside these ranges, but we're just being strict in order to shortlist.

If the full market reports look too intimidating at first, then use the table at the top called 'industrial and resource leaders'. There's only 150 (ish) of them.

Note: Industrial and resource leaders are not published separately in Monday's *Financial Review*.

Additional notes

- At times of depressed markets, plenty of shares will have franked dividends with yields higher than 7%, so if you find yourself headed for a long list, just increase your cut-off yield at a higher percentage like 8% to 10%, and if you're still having trouble then just look up the dividend yields for blue chips like Coles Myer, Telstra and Commonwealth Bank, take the average and add 3% to get a reasonable cut-off percentage.

- If companies don't have dividend yields reported—if they're just marked with a dash—skip them this time round. Also skip mining and oil companies which don't pay dividends. At this stage, you can afford to be fussy.

- Abnormally high yields are not always suspicious. High yields are not a promise of what future dividends will be. They're an indication of what they will be like if you buy at today's price AND the next dividend is the same as the last one. If the share price has plummeted since the dividend was paid, or if an abnormal profit distribution was made to shareholders, then the dividend yield will look unusually high. There's still little point considering these shares for your shortlist, since unusually big dividends are rarely paid two reporting periods in a row. Also, companies whose share price has plummeted that much in the last six months are less likely to declare a decent dividend next time without the profits to pay for them.

STEP 4: A DECENT SHARE PRICE

Look at the last sale price. Is it under $7?

If over $7, forget it for now. Go back to scanning down the dividend yield column at step 1.

If under $7, look at the 52-week highs and lows.

Is the last sale price about 10% or more above the lowest AND 30% or more below the top price?

If *no*, put an asterisk next to this company in case you want to look at it again later or keep an eye on it for a while.

If *yes*, it has potential for a good recovery. Go to step 5.

Note: Yes, you are bypassing a lot of blue chip shares that cost more than $7. But there's so much opportunity out there, you have to draw the line somewhere.

The lower your share price, the greater the effect that an increase of every single cent can have on your percentage growth. For example, for every 1000 shares bought at $10, a one cent increase in share price equals capital growth of only 0.001%. But if you only paid $1 a share for 1000 shares which went up one cent, your investment would grow by 0.1%—100 times faster!

STEP 5: COMPARING NTA (NTA = NET TANGIBLE ASSETS)

If you're worried about companies going bust and taking your investment with them, look for companies with net tangible asset values as close as possible to (or over) the last sale price.

Notes: Stockmarket shares—contrary to rumour—have a certain level of guarantee on your capital investment. It's measured largely by the NTA.

The NTA is your security blanket. It gives you a fair idea of how much you'd get back for every ordinary share you own if the company had to sell off all its assets and pay off all its debts.

If the NTA is higher than the share price, add it to your list now AND add an asterisk to give it special attention when you research. This could be your bargain buy.

As your confidence and portfolio grows, you can let the NTA slide down your priorities list, if you wish.

Note: Companies that don't need big assets to function—like banks, travel agents and information technologists—often have much smaller NTAs. The share price is valued high on other things instead, like reputation and potential for profits.

There's nothing wrong with buying a company with a tiny NTA compared to its share price—just that you must be aware that you're unlikely to get as much of your money back if they go bust.

When you do look at NTAs of various companies, make sure you compare like with like. It would be unfair to compare a company like Flight Centre—which has very little in the way of tangible assets—with a high asset-owning company like Coates Hire, based on the NTA values or P/E ratios alone. You'll get a much truer picture of how a company is performing within its own marketplace by comparing its statistics with those of its competitors.

STEP 6: P/E RATIO

To start your portfolio, you're looking for P/E ratios between 6 and 14. *Please note*: You can still make good money on stocks with P/E ratios lower than 6 or higher than 14—but you do it at a much greater risk.

Note: Resource stocks—the mining companies etc.—do not always have P/E ratios published. Don't sweat it. The figures aren't available—usually because they haven't reported yet, or because they're in the process of moving from loss-making into profit-making. Either way, L-plate investors won't be interested in resource stocks that don't have published P/E ratios, because there are already stacks of companies to choose from AND you shouldn't invest in anything where you can't get all the info.

STEP 7: EPS (EARNINGS PER SHARE)

Glance at the EPS column.

If the EPS is positive, *you now add this company to your list.*

If the EPS value is negative AND the P/E is under 6, the company is still recording losses with little hope for recovery soon. Pass it by.

If the EPS value is negative BUT the P/E is between 6 and 14, OR if you've already added this company at step 5 with an asterisk, *then add it to your shortlist now,* but research thoroughly to find out what the problem is. (Is it management or the state of the market that's at fault?)

> Jot down as many companies as you like, provided they fulfill all of the criteria in steps 1 to 7, completing each column of your table as you go.

Notes: Resource stocks—like oil, gas, gold and other mining companies—do not publish EPS values. That's not a bad thing. Just use the P/E ratio and other points in this checklist to compare them.

A high EPS (say 30% or more of their share price) is a good thing. If companies are making good profits, their share price can't stay low for long, unless they have some serious problems to deal with. Also, high EPS companies sometimes tend to pay bigger dividends next time round.

Use the EPS to compare companies on your short-list when deciding which company is the most likely to succeed in the medium to long term.

Your shortlist is now complete. On to the last stages . . .

STEP 8: TIME FOR A CLOSER LOOK

This is where the more detailed research begins. Don't groan. It could be the most financially rewarding work you ever do. You spend every weekday slogging your guts out for your boss. Why not recharge your coffee cup, grab another couple of biscuits (brain food) and curl up for a quiet half hour with your telephone? Work for yourself for a change.

You only need to ring your stockbroker, the best three to six companies on your shortlist—and maybe if you're keen, check the net. Here's how:

YOUR STOCKBROKER

Possibly the best source of up-to-date info at your 'phone-tips'. If there's any gossip, they usually know about it.

Better than gossip, they have up-to-the-minute statistics. They have regular meetings to keep everyone in their staff up to date, as well as office circulars, email bulletins, ASX newsflashes and media releases, not to mention good old-fashioned market observations by their dedicated teams of company researchers.

Don't bother ringing and blurting out their nightmare question: 'Well, Mary, which company is a bargain today?' After making it through the first five steps of this chapter, you should be wise enough to realise that bargains are different for everyone—depending on your individual portfolio goals—and the opportunities are so vast even then, it would take an entire day just to list them on the telephone. Instead, run through the companies that have made your shortlist. Doing it this way means your stockbroker will look forward to your calls instead of dreading them.

QUESTIONS FOR YOUR STOCKBROKER

Ask Mary what your shortlisted companies do, if you don't already know. What do they sell or supply? Are they national/international or do they operate from one small office filled with computers which could easily disappear overnight? Ask if the major shareholders are made up of largely notable big investors like superannuation funds and banks, or with original directors who still retain the majority of ownership?

Ask her what she thinks of each of them, discussing their 52-week highs and lows, because she has the exact dates of these on her database. She can also usually tell you at least roughly *why* they occurred when they did.

Ask her about management. Are the companies on your shortlist run by a dedicated and professional team, with practical experience that actually relates to their particular company? (Don't laugh. You'd be surprised how many companies are run by directors with theoretical experience only. Some are sports stars. Others are ex-politicians—although the occasional ex-pollie can actually be an interesting asset to a company because of their broad networks of not-so-ex-business contacts.)

Watch out for trouble at the top

I once owned shares in an engineering company that had performed extremely well—until dissent broke out in the ranks of the directors. There was a long and ugly campaign to vote out two of the longest serving directors who were both engineers, and eventually the company was left with directors who were all accountants. I sold my shares soon afterwards and wasn't sorry. The share price fell just as fast as the profits and the company is still struggling three years later.

Before you hang up—and now that Mary has an idea of what you're looking for—ask her if she thinks you've overlooked any companies that could outperform the ones on your shortlist.

Get your broker's recommendation, and then advise her you'll be *calling back* with a decision as soon as you can. (Don't worry if that's in a few days, instead of later that day.) Also . . .

CHECK THE INTERNET

- Check the archived and latest media releases on the ASX website (www.asx.com.au) for the latest announcements by the companies on your shortlist.
- Check the Reserve Bank of Australia website (www. rba.gov.au) for media releases on general government policy changes, which might affect certain industries or markets.
- Check the *Australian Financial Review* website (www.afr. com.au) for latest announcements and archived reports on your companies. (Subscription costs apply to most reports on this site.)
- Check the Australian Shareholders' Association website for free investor watchdog information:
  www.asa.asn.au/Default.htm or phone 1300 368 448. (Annual membership if you wish is $66 for newsletters etc.)
- Check the home pages of each company on your shortlist to find: share price graphs, recent news, contact details, and annual reports if available via the net.
- Even if you can find all the information you need through your stockbroker and internet, it is still always interesting to contact the head office of the company yourself.

Note: If you don't have internet access, don't sweat. You can find out all you need to know by:

CONTACTING THE COMPANY

Put on your Sherlock Holmes hat. This is where you get to have some fun. You're about to become a part-owner in a company employing hundreds, sometimes thousands, of people. Obviously, it would be silly not to learn more about it. What does it do? Is it a small niche marketer, or a strong leader in a major industry?

Yes, you can do this on the internet via the company website too, but the telephone is often the best method, I think, because it's personal. Occasionally you even get a secretary who puts you through to one of the board of directors—which is usually a sign that the company is much smaller than you may have thought.

Calling two or three companies—even interstate—doesn't have to be expensive as many have toll-free numbers. But even if they don't, you're not talking for long and these STD calls are tax-deductible as home-office expenses for managing your investments. (You'd be flat strap spending $20 in research calls.)

HERE'S WHAT YOU'RE LOOKING FOR IN THE COMPANY

- Are their phone staff happy, courteous, efficient and do they seem to have pride in their company?
- Try to involve staff in relaxed conversations. Ask them briefly about their directors. Do they treat their staff well? Do they try to keep trained employees from resigning by granting paid maternity leave, instituting employee share plans or other incentives?
- Ask about their head office. Ask them to describe it. Look for pictures of it on the net or in annual reports. Is it overly flashy? Is it conservative, yet professional? Or is it the corporate equivalent of the back of someone's garage?
- Ask for a prospectus or latest annual report—even if you have all the information already—just to test their efficiency, by seeing how long it takes to get to you. (One company once took 11 months to reply. No wonder their share price crashed!)
- When and where is their annual general meeting held? Does it seem deliberately hard to get to?
- Is the annual report or the prospectus easy to read? Is it overly glossy, complicated or vague?

READING ANNUAL REPORTS

You don't have to be a genius to see where all the money's coming from. Just run your finger down the money columns in the back of the annual reports and read the details beside the biggest amounts. (If the report is nearly a year old, check current market statistics to see if their predictions for the last year were correct—this tells you if they're meeting their goals.)

Also use annual reports to:

- Look at level of borrowings (also known as gearing/gearing ratio).

If gearing ratio is 50% or less, this is okay. It's common and considered safe.

If gearing ratio is between 50% and 100%, you need to search thoroughly for important announcements which could change the company's ability to earn profits or pay dividends.

If gearing ratio is 100% or more, this is a warning to investigate even more thoroughly or NOT to invest in the company at this time.

- Can you see where they make their biggest profits? As suggested, it should be obvious in the annual summaries in the back of the annual report—even to the untrained eye. If it's not, then be suspicious. Be very suspicious.
- Read the auditor's report near the end of the annual report. Auditors are obliged by law to be impartial and report any findings which may affect the shareholders or their decisions to buy, sell or hold their investments in that company.
- Do the directors hold directorships with many other companies? (It's frighteningly common to see people appointed to the boards of between six and ten different companies at a time, and I can't help but wonder how they can possibly have the time to do their best for every one.) Also look at their pay packages.
- Do they have—or are they planning—any shareholder discounts for themselves and their employees? If so, they're trying to keep their talented staff for long periods.
- Also check how often the company assets are valued. Their forecasts could be based on outdated records.

STEP 9: THE FINAL DOUBLE CHECK

Compare your shortlisted companies with each other and select the ones that have the best potential for improvement, best reputation for maintaining high dividends, and best customer/investor relations.

Congratulations, you're through all the hard stuff. Now you just have to look through your shortlist. The top three finalists should be leaping off the page at you. If not, you can narrow your choices further by crossing off any companies that don't quite measure up at each step.

Occasionally—during a crash for instance—bargains start popping up everywhere, so you could end up with two or three really close contenders on your shortlist. If you have $5000 or more to invest, then pick two or more companies to invest in, spreading the risk by improving the depth of your portfolio.

Otherwise, since your finalists have all made it this far through your selection process, then it's fairly safe now to eenie-meenie-minie-moe yourself a final choice.

Course of sales reports: A few pages after the share price reports in the *Financial Review* (about once a week) is a page and a half of minuscule fine print called the course of sales report. Don't panic. I'm not asking you to read it from start to finish. Heck, you don't have to read it at all, if that's your choice. But you'll be missing out on a nifty little trick that only small investors can take advantage of.

Use this report to watch companies on your shortlist for a few days at least before you buy them. It gives you an idea of what you can expect the highest and lowest to be the next day if there are no upsets.

For example, here's a magnified sample course of sales report from the *Australian Financial Review*, Wednesday, 26 July 2000. (Statistics always are for the previous day's trading.):

Coles Myer 675 675 672 675 672 674 672 673 671 673 671 673 672 673 672 673 672 673 672 673 672 673 672 673 672 673 672 673 672 669 671 669 670 669 670 669 670 669 670 669 670 669 670 (4215713)

Here, Coles Myer shares are shown in cents, so 675 translates to $6.75. The figure in brackets at the end is the total number of shares sold the previous day. At a glance you can see any trends in price fluctuations almost as easily as using a computer program.

L-plate investors should watch the stock for three or four days *at least* before placing a buy order for shares through either their virtual or two-legged brokers. (Monday's and Friday's movements are less predictable because big investors get a bit frantic sometimes over news that breaks—or might break—over the weekend.)

FOR SMALL INVESTORS ONLY

Obviously, in a steadily rising market, you'll have more luck finding a $10 bill with your face on it than finding a seller who'll accept less than the market rate for their shares. But in most other markets, small investors can use the following trick to get better value for their buying dollar.

Trick for a slow-falling, static or slow-rising market: If there's hope of a recovery soon, try using your course of sales report to predict what two or three days worth of repeated drop is worth and try placing a small 'at limit' offer that's this much lower than the last day's close. At limit orders sit in your stockbroker's records for up to a week—depending on the broker—waiting for the price to be achieved. So while you're busily distracted at work a few days later, you can often bag a small bargain, even if the markets rise.

STEP 10: CRUNCH TIME, MAKING THE CALL

Call your stockbroker back, make sure there are no last minute media announcements that might affect your decision to buy, and then place your order and make arrangements to send the money within three days of the transaction.

Then open a bottle of your favourite tipple, because now it's time to celebrate. *You just bought a company*. Well, part of one.

WHY PRICES FLUCTUATE

Share prices go up—like prices for anything—when there are more buyers than sellers. And they go down when sellers need to drop their price to attract a buyer. Mostly, it's that simple.

Sometimes, however, large investment houses or even the companies themselves dump large share parcels on the market to sell, driving the price down temporarily. At other times, companies or major investors may try to increase shareholdings in a particular company, temporarily causing a demand which inflicts price rises.

Other major influences include Christmas trading, end of financial years and anticipation of good or bad profit results just before they're announced. Price fluctuations are not something to fear. They are to be expected, and once you've got a handle on that idea you'll look forward to market crashes instead of dreading them, as this is when the best bargains appear.

PREDICTING THE FUTURE

L-platers can't hope to predict market cycles or fluctuations exactly. But they can get a fair idea of how things tend to flow, based on historical trends.

I put together the following chart a few years ago to help me get things straight in my head. Yes, it's oversimplified. But it's also fairly reliable. I adapted the information from a study of trade cycles over a 150-year period and overlaid employment trends and then presented it so it's not nearly so scary to look at.

At a glance, you can see the changes in the economy that can be triggered by other market forces. Reading clockwise, for example, falling share prices can lead to falling commodity prices; falling commodities lead eventually to cheaper real estate; and so on round the cycle.

These trends are not gospel. Governments and the Reserve Bank can manipulate certain aspects to forcibly drive the market in a desired direction. Dropping interest rates a few months before an election, for example, often results in a timely drop in unemployment.

Use this chart to help you judge the best times to buy or sell ANY kind of investment

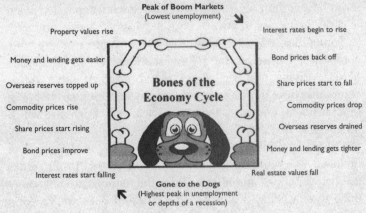

Peak of Boom Markets
(Lowest unemployment)

Property values rise

Money and lending gets easier

Overseas reserves topped up

Commodity prices rise

Share prices start rising

Bond prices improve

Interest rates start falling

Interest rates begin to rise

Bond prices back off

Share prices start to fall

Commodity prices drop

Overseas reserves drained

Money and lending gets tighter

Real estate values fall

Bones of the Economy Cycle

Gone to the Dogs
(Highest peak in unemployment
or depths of a recession)

POSITIVE INDICATORS

For buying:

- As shown in the previous section, one good sign that the sharemarket is generally about to rise is a drop in interest rates followed by a rise in bond prices—both of which are commented on regularly in the business sections of any good newspaper.
- Blue chips are shares that are listed in the 150 market leaders. If one of these companies makes it into your short-list it's usually a good opportunity to buy, even if they're experiencing management problems, because blue chips are heavily owned by major investors who have enough combined votes to gang up on management and force them to perform better—or else!

For selling:

- If interest rates start to rise AND bond prices start to back off, it's a signal to watch your share prices carefully. If you're investing for the long term, a cycle-down in the stockmarket will hardly make you blink. Why sell now, if you'll only have to pay tax on it? If, however, you've got some shares which have outgrown the safe P/E ratio range AND they're settling around their 52-week highs, then perhaps you should consider selling those shares, parking the cash in your mortgage offset account, credit card, or term deposit for a while, and keeping an eye out for the next bargain to appear on your shortlist.

WARNING SIGNS (one last chance to see if you are really a shareholder at heart.)

Obviously, every investment carries some degree of risk—yes, even term deposits. The object of investing is to maximise your return, while keeping your risk at a minimum. But don't get paranoid. It's only money and the level of risk you choose has to be something you can sleep with at nights.

If you have $2000 or more—but you're still not convinced about trading generally in your own shares—consider buying bonds, debentures or blue chip shares instead; their returns are orgasmically better than goal savings accounts or term deposits.

DON'T be put off by the 'I know someone who knows someone else who got burned once' stories that float around. But DO be suspicious of seductive promises of high returns.

Warning Sign 1: If the promised return on investment is more than twice the current interest rate you're paying on your home loan, then look for a catch.

Warning 2: Beware of rumours, tips and apparent 'inside information'. These days, company directors are required to inform the stock exchange immediately when making any decision that may affect the company's share price on the market.

WHEN TO SELL?

You only sell shares when:
• you need the money (hopefully for nothing trivial)
OR
• when you have a company that's broken through its 52-week high AND is starting to settle down AND you spot another

bargain which you expect to cycle upwards in the next few months AND you don't mind paying tax on any capital gain that year

OR

• when your shares have exceeded goals AND are slowing because interest rates have started to rise AND bond prices are backing off sharply. Do your maths to see if you should cash your shares and park them in your mortgage offset account, or a few term deposits, until interest rates fall again, or until the market accepts the interest rate and starts climbing again with inflation.

SHOULD YOU BORROW TO INVEST?

No, if you can't afford the repayments out of your salary or paypacket, and have to rely on investment income to make ends meet. Sometimes you can set up your loans so the repayments rely on you being paid dividends or by selling shares as the prices rise. But L-plate investors can get themselves into serious hot water by being forced to sell shares for a loss, just to make your repayments. Don't borrow what you can't repay by yourself.

Yes, if you can afford repayments by yourself out of your normal pay AND if you wish to negative-gear the interest so you can buy bigger parcels of shares (to make your investment grow faster) AND if you've reached the point as an investor where you know what you're doing.

SHARES PAPERWORK: RECORD-KEEPING FOR THE BONE LAZY OR BUSY

Blechhhh! Paperwork. If you've read my first book, you'll probably remember what I think about paperwork.

Yes, some brokers offer management services, but for goodness' sake, ask about the cost before you agree. All the paperwork—CHESS statements (see Shares Jargon), buy and sell orders and dividend statements—usually get sent to your home address anyway, so you still have filing to do (about as much as filing your phone, rates and power bills). The rest of the record-keeping is easy.

Just keep a simple list which sets out details of what you bought or sold each financial year, including share prices and how many dividends were paid to you and how many were re-invested in DRPs. Don't pay big fees for something that is little more than a computer-generated printout. Also, letting the management of your investments slip from your hands can be expensive to your portfolio. You might as well go for managed funds and cop all the costs that go with them.

A FINAL WORD

As I said, managing your shares is easy. Most of the time, you're just keeping one sleepy eye on what they're up to—and grinning at their progress.

It's much the same principle as I recommend for budgeting actually. After all, it's only money. Your spare time is best spent with your friends and family—having fun, not slaving over figures.

So go on. Whether you're starting out or starting over, you now know everything you need to, to get things straight.

Get out there and get into it.

This is where the fun begins!

Appendix I

Income

On this page, list and add up all your fortnightly (or weekly/ monthly) income, but don't include any bank interest or hobby income at this stage, unless you regularly rely on these amounts to survive from pay to pay.

Income source or employer	Amount per f/n ($)
_____	_____
_____	_____
_____	_____
_____	_____
_____	_____
_____	_____

Total income per pay = $_____.___

Appendix II

Current Urgent Debts

On this page, list everyone to whom you currently owe money, and should have repaid, but haven't yet because you haven't been able to afford it. Include only those debts which should have been paid already (outstanding debts) to friends, family, credit cards, laybys, banks, landlords, money-lenders and other finance or rental companies, but don't worry about your regular payments to any of these groups yet, because you'll be taking care of them in Appendix III.

Item	$Total owing	$Minimum repayment	Due date	Comments	Urgency rating
Credit Card					
Layby at:					
Overdue Bills:					
IOUs:					
Other:					
TOTALS:	$	$			

Appendix III

Predictable Expenditure

Use this table to list all your major and minor predictable expenses for the year. Check old bills to see how much you paid last time, but make sure to update them for any price increases that may have occurred since then. Round each figure up to the nearest dollar—or even five dollars—if you like to provide a safety net.

Bills	$ per year	$ per f/nly pay
ANNUAL LIVING EXPENSES		
rates = $ by times per year		
phone (home, mobile) and internet access		
electricity/gas		
car registration		
car insurance		
car repairs / servicing (on average over last five years)*		
house, contents, health & car insurance		
school books & other public education costs		
meat, clothes & haircuts if purchased in bulk		
medical: contraception, gym fees, vitamins & medicines		

union fees		
vet shots, worming, flea treatments etc.		
savings for Christmas/holidays/furniture		
(You can work this out in the fortnightly column if you prefer… eg. put either $520 in the year column or $20 in the /FN column.)		
Sub-total: annual expenses:	$	
which rounds up to a fortnightly cost so far of:		$
+ OUT OF POCKET EXPENSES PER FORTNIGHT:		
mortgage payment/house rent/housekeeping contribution		
credit card repayment including extra for interest		
(Note: This is NOT your minimum repayment. It's how much you need to pay in order to pay off your credit card in a few months—not a few years!)		
car and other loans		
whitegoods rental if any		
meat & groceries		
buses, taxi fares & trains		
meals at work		
pocketmoney for children		
union fees (if automatically deducted from paypacket)		
Christmas & other savings if not already included.		
regular hobbies/sports		
other (including newspapers/magazines/lotto/takeaway meals etc.)		
Sub-total expenses per fortnight:		$
add a safety net for inflation and round up:		$
= Total basic living expenses per fortnight:		$

*If you have no idea how much you've spent on car repairs, maintenance and servicing in the last five years, then you can try the following amounts as a guide, until you have a better idea of expenses for your own car: 0-5 year-old car: $300 a year; 5-10 year-old car: $800 a year; 10-year-or-older car: $1500 a year.

Appendix IV

Your Sanity Allowance

Note: I chose $40 here because it's roughly the equivalent of a week's worth of fuel. Choose an amount that suits you—hopefully less than $50 a week.

UNDER $40	OVER $40
eg. A video-fest with friends	eg. A day at the footy with the kids

Appendix V

Keeping Track of your Sanity Allowance and Savings

Use this table to keep track of your savings so you can save for multiple purposes at the same time.

Note: You don't need to bother keeping running totals. Just fill in your goal and how much you're saving each pay towards it at the top of the column and then tick off each pay as the money gets automatically transferred into your account. If you ever need to know how much you've got saved in the meantime, just add up the value of the ticks, being careful if some ticks are worth more than others in neighbouring columns.

Goals/Savings List

Pay date	$ /pay	$ /pay	$ /pay	$ /pay	$ /pay	$ /pay
Approx. cost	$	$	$	$	$	$

Appendix VI

Pennies from Heaven: Are you Eligible?

Like pennies from heaven the Commonwealth government pours funds through Centrelink to provide various payments and allowances to help Australians survive financially under every kind of hardship you can imagine. Although many people argue that it's never enough, the mind still boggles at the amount of effort it takes to ensure that every one of us has this safety net under us. When you learn how to survive (and sometimes thrive) on a low income, it becomes even more reassuring to know that it's there. (And it can make you feel better about paying your taxes.)

The list of all payments available is too long to publish here. You can access the a-z listing on the Centrelink website www.centrelink.gov.au and if you don't have access to a PC at home, you can get free access to the website at your local job network provider Centrelink-approved employment agency or by contacting them by using the numbers in Appendix VII.

This appendix is worth reading, **even if none of it applies to you**, because it's highly likely that you will know another Aussie battler who is entitled to an income supplement but has no idea that they are. So please skim through these segments anyway and **spread the word** to those you care about.

YOUTH ALLOWANCE

YA is for young adults up to age 21 who need financial assistance while they're studying, training or looking for a job. To get YA you either need to stay at school, or go back to school, or get into a TAFE or another approved training course, or be specifically exempted from this requirement.

If you're 16 or 17 AND leave school without finishing Year 12 AND if you can't find a job, you'll need to satisfy an Activity Agreement with Centrelink before you can receive Youth Allowance (unless you're severely disadvantaged). That means you'll be asked to do some kind of studying or training. And yes, it is intended to make it harder for you to drop out.

Unless your parents give permission for it to be paid into your account, YA usually gets paid to them. It IS subject to various income and assets tests, so it can go down if you work (or if you're living away from home and have a partner who works), or if your parents' combined income is over $28,000, or if they own over $424,750 in assets (excluding the family home and up to 2 hectares of land). It can also be increased if there are other kids in your family.

HOW MUCH IS YA?
If you're living at home and:
- under 18, the basic YA rate is currently $153.90 per fortnight.
- aged 18–21, the basic YA rate is $185.00 per fortnight.

If you're living away from home, basic YA is $281.10 per fortnight. Yes—strangely—it still depends on how much your parents earn, on the assumption that your parents are still helping you out financially, even when you're not living with them, but the cut-offs and sliding scales are different.

For more information on YA, contact Centrelink on 13 24 90 or to discuss the various income and asset tests, call 13 10 21.

On top of Youth Allowance, you can also apply for Rural and Remote Allowance (in which case you can also apply for higher income support payments) and Fares Allowance if you have to travel to study or to get to work. (If you're renting, you may also be entitled to Rent Assistance.)

Many rural districts are within comfortable commuting distance of metropolitan areas, so it may be worthwhile moving in with your country cousins—or renting just over the district boundary—until you find your financial feet.

Handy hint: Full-time students can sometimes average their income—eg. if they earn heaps over the holidays, and then nothing all term—by using what Centrelink calls an 'Income Bank'. It's a way of smoothing out the repercussions that your unreliable income might have on your Centrelink payments, so if you are forced to work in dribs and drabs contact Centrelink as above for an application form and further details.

NEWSTART (JOB SEARCH) ALLOWANCE FOR THE UNEMPLOYED

Eligibility and entitlements for this payment (once called unemployment benefits) are now conditional to unemployed people over 21 years of age but under pension age.

Conditions are many but include requirements that you have to be registered with Centrelink and you have to apply fortnightly in person. They do grant concessions for you to fax your applications in if you're rural or sick or in training, but you have to get permission in advance.

You also have to sign a 'Mutual Obligations' agreement committing you to apply for jobs regularly, and you have to pass their activity test every fortnight with the information you supply on your fortnightly application.

Rates are currently:

$350.80 per fortnight if you're single, 21 or over, and have no kids.

$379.30 if you're single, 21 or over, but have children.

$316.40 if you have a partner.

Newstart is subject to an income test as well as an asset test, and in addition to the payments, you may also be entitled to rent assistance, a health care card (which entitles you to various discounts) and additional payments as follows:

- Once only Employment Entry Payment of $104
- Once only Education Entry Payment of $208
- Pharmaceutical Allowance if you get sick while you're on Newstart (medical certificate required).

> **Newstart usually has a minimum one-week waiting period.**

If you participate in the 'Work for the Dole' program, you can also be eligible for an additional payment of $20.80 a fortnight while you're involved.

> **Advances of allowance up to $500 may be available (for almost any Centrelink payment actually), but be careful not to blow this money on trivial purchases because your Centrelink payment will be reduced until it's paid back.**

You are NOT entitled to Newstart Allowance if you've been doing seasonal work; or if you're on strike or been laid off because of industrial action; or if you've been paid out your leave entitlements from your last job—in this case you have to wait until these 'virtual' holidays are over. You also have to exhaust any funds that Centrelink deems to be 'reasonably' available to you already. And you can't move to an area where you'll have less chance of getting a job.

Handy hint 1: You CAN get Newstart paid to you if you're a mother who decides to return to the workforce even if you have a spouse who works and even if your partner has been supporting you for years. Your partner's income will be means-tested to determine how much you get, but if you think you would like to rejoin the workforce, you are entitled to apply for Newstart payments as soon as you make the decision.

Handy hint 2: If you have a good relationship with your new employer, and if you suspect that industrial action is pending but you can't afford to be laid off, first contact your union to see if they run a contingency fund to help support you while you're on strike. If not, and if you risk extreme financial hardship by full participation in the strike, discuss the matter with your employer and ask them to advance you paid holidays for the period, in lieu of holidays you will be due later. Most full-time jobs accrue paid holidays at the rate of 1.5 days a month, so if—for example—you've been working two months, you technically have about three days paid holiday up your sleeve. You're still technically supporting the strike because production stops while you're away, and you're still making a sacrifice for the union because your holidays are castrated later. (Of course, some of your workmates might not see it that way.)

Note: Casual jobs don't accrue holidays. You get paid a higher hourly rate instead.

Handy hint 3: You can still get paid Newstart—even if you've started working part-time or casual, although the amount you get is means-tested so it may be reduced.

TO APPLY FOR NEWSTART
Ring Centrelink on 13 28 50. You'll need proof of your identity and age, your address and details of your income and assets. If you've worked in the last 12 months you'll also need the 'Employment Separation Certificate' from your last employer. If you didn't get one, ask them for one and if they give you trouble, advise Centrelink immediately.

Once Newstart is approved, Centrelink will explain how to

fill in a Job Seeker Diary and advise you when you need to provide them with Employer Contact Certificates (as evidence that you've attempted to find work).

If you've been unfit for work for more than 12 months, your situation will be reviewed. If you are likely to be permanently unable to work, you may qualify for a Disability Support Pension.

Reviews: Newstart can be reviewed at any time on top of the scheduled three-monthly reviews. Following reviews, you may be asked to start training courses or attend interviews to help get you into the workforce before more payments can be made.

Warning: If you move to a new address where employment hopes are more slender, payments can stop for up to six months as a punishment! If you have to move because your landlord kicks you out, make sure you ring Centrelink to confirm your new area is okay before you commit to a new landlord—just to be sure.

JOB SEARCH TRAINING

While you're earning Newstart Allowance, you can be asked to do job search training, aimed at improving your job search skills, motivation and opportunities. Training is usually individually tailored to suit you and will include help with writing and preparing résumés and job applications, getting references, approaching employers and developing interviewing skills. Training is for three to four weeks and may involve further reviews.

DISABILITY SUPPORT PENSION

The Disability Support Pension is available to *anyone* aged 16 to 55 if you're unable to work because of a serious health problem—yes, even if you're still studying—just so long as your disability or serious health problem has lasted—or is likely to last—for two years or more AND if you can't work more than 30 hours a week because of it. Naturally, this has to be certified by your doctor, who will provide you with a medical certificate and doctor's report to forward with your DSP application.

The DSP is a maximum of $313.20 per fortnight, and yes, it does reduce in accordance with your partner's income, and is subject to an assets test (unless you're permanently blind, in which case special rules apply).

Mothers who decide to return to work after raising children but who discover they can't because of nagging health problems—like chronic arthritis or asthma—seem to be the most likely people to miss out on applying for DSP. The thought often doesn't occur to them because they're used to being dependent on their husbands. So if you know anyone like this, make sure they realise their entitlements.

Yes, DSP does get reviewed regularly—usually at least every two to five years—and you may be sent to a government doctor for a second opinion at almost any time. Naturally, payouts you get from workers' compensation, third party damages or lump sum payouts from health insurance may also affect your entitlements. Contact Centrelink about these BEFORE you receive or spend the extra money.

CARER'S PAYMENT

Carer's Payment helps you care for your adult children, your spouse or your parents in their own home (or alternatively in your home) if they are unable to look after themselves because of severe health or psychiatric problems or because of disability. Various conditions apply and you can only get a Carer's Payment if you work less than 20 hours a week.

The Carer's Payment is currently $394.10 or $328.90 each if you're looking after two or more people—for instance, your parents. It's subject to both income and asset tests, it's reviewed regularly and other conditions apply because you also get a Pensioner Concession Card. Contact 13 27 17 for more information.

There is also a Return to Work Program to help people get back into the workforce if they want to after giving up work for two years or more to look after family members who needed it. The Return to Work hotline is 1300 363 037.

CHILDCARE BENEFIT

This payment helps you pay for various forms of childcare, including family or long day care, as well as occasional, vacation or registered care and childcare after school hours. The childcare provider has to be approved or registered (with the Family Assistance Office) and you must pay childcare fees in order to claim the benefit payments.

Yes, you could pay fees to your parents to care for your children while you're working—some grandparents then bank the fees into trust accounts for their grandchildren's education or use the money for outings and play materials—but your parents would have to be approved carers and declare the income for their pension if applicable. Other conditions also apply. Call the Family Assistance Office at Centrelink on 13 61 50 for more information.

Note: Payments are subject to an income test (but not an asset test) and they can be paid either directly to the childcare provider or to you as a lump sum at the end of the financial year.

For approved childcare providers, you can get up to $122 per week for under-school-age kids that need 50 hours of care and 85% of that for school-aged kids. Rules are a little more complicated for registered childcare providers, and you have to pay first and show receipts.

Handy hint: Rural (and some metro fringe) childcare providers are exempt from the 50 hours rule, so consider this when choosing a place to live. Living just outside metropolitan areas for childcare purposes can make working life more flexible.

> If you're entitled to Childcare Benefit, you could also be entitled to Parenting Payment (if you're the main caregiver); Family Tax Benefit; Maternity Allowance (after the birth of your baby); or Maternity Immunisation Allowance (for 18-month-old children who've been fully immunised or been granted exemption).

MATERNITY ALLOWANCE: UP TO $780 PER BIRTH

Paid to you after you 'pop' a new baby, or adopt one that's under 26 weeks of age, this allowance may also be payable if your baby is stillborn or dies soon after birth (in which case, you may also be entitled to bereavement allowance).

You apply for MA using the same form that you use to apply for the Family Tax Benefit, which is available from Centrelink on 13 61 50 or from the nurse or social worker at your hospital.

MA is a non-taxable lump sum once-off payment of up to $780 per birth—so double or triple that if you pop twins or triplets—usually paid promptly. It is subject to an income test, but not an asset test.

MATERNITY IMMUNISATION ALLOWANCE: $208

If your child was born after January 1998, you can claim this allowance when your bundle of joy reaches 18 months old and has either been fully immunised or has been granted an exemption. You have to be eligible for Family Tax Benefit A or been paid the Maternity Allowance detailed above AND you have to make your application before bumpkin's second birthday to get it, but under these circumstances you may also be able to claim it if your baby is stillborn or dies before it's 18 months old. Currently, the non-taxable lump sum once-off payment is $208. It IS subject to an income test but not an asset test.

OTHER PAYMENTS

Centrelink provides various other payments to help you through extra-severe financial hardships. Some of these not already mentioned include:

- **Crisis Payment**—if you're forced out of your house because of fire or domestic violence, or if you've suffered severe financial hardship after being in jail for more than two weeks.
- **Bereavement Payments**—to help you adjust to changed financial circumstances after the death of your partner, carer or young child.
- **Isolated Children Assistance**—to help get your remote-area kids to school.
- **Family Tax Benefit Part A**—to help you with the costs of raising children.
- **Family Tax Benefit Part B**—supplement payment usually for single income or sole parent families.

Centrelink: Note—Centrelink call lines operate Monday to Friday 8.00am–5.00pm. (www.centrelink.com.au)

Appointments:	13 1021
Customer Relations:	1800 050 004
Centrelink Multilingual Call:	13 1202
TTY:	1800 810 586
Employment Services:	13 2850
Retirement Services:	13 2300
Disability, Sickness and Carers:	13 2717

(Centrelink Family Assistance Office is open 8.00am–8.00pm Monday to Friday and waiting times are often shortest Tuesday, Wednesday and Friday afternoons. Mornings and the first day after a public holiday, they're usually flat strap.)

Appendix VII

Useful Contacts
(Where to go when you need free help)

- Countrylink is a free government referral service to government and community services throughout the country. They give you some contact phone numbers of where to start looking when you have no idea which government department can help you with your problems. Phone 1800 026 222. All they ask is the postcode you're calling from so they can keep track of who's using their service.
- Also try these contact phone numbers (current at time of publication):

Family Assistance Office:	13 6150
Youth and Students:	13 2490
ABSTUDY:	13 2317
Isolated Children:	13 2318
Employer Contact Unit:	13 1158
Moving Overseas:	1800 050 041
Calling from overseas:	+613 6222 3455
Social security arrangements with other countries:	13 1673

Australian Tax Office (ATO)

Free accounting program (e-record, developed for reporting
GST):   13 2478
General inquiries: 13 2861
GST publications: 13 3038
Savings bonus for older Aussies: 13 2862
GST private inquiries: 13 6320
Tax file number applications: 13 2863
GST business inquiries: 13 2478
Check progress of your tax return: 13 2863
Debt collection (for tax debts you can't afford to pay): 13 2550

Commonwealth Ombudsman: If you have a complaint about a Commonwealth government department that you can't get fixed no matter how hard you try by dealing directly with the department involved: 1300 362 072 (website: www.comb.gov.au).

Privacy Commissioner: If you're worried that your tax details have not been treated confidentially: 1300 363 992 (website: www.privacy.gov.au).

The Australian Stock Exchange (ASX) offers an excellent range of free and low-cost information and regular seminars to educate Australia's growing population of potential and existing shareholders. For details, see their website at www.asx.com.au; email: info@asx.com.au; phone: 1300 300 279.

Appendix VIII

Shares Jargon

All Ordinaries Index: aka the Share Price Index (SPI), is calculated on the share prices of over 270 ASX listed Aussie companies. Although you can now invest in the SPI itself on the Futures Exchange, the All Ordinaries should be used by beginners as a guide only to how the market in general traded on that day. A major dive in price of only one blue chip can plummet the All Ordinaries, when in fact all other companies are doing just fine.

At Discretion: when you tell your stockbroker they can buy/sell your shares at the best price they think they can get for you (within a week, usually).

At Limit: when you tell your stockbroker the highest price you're prepared to pay or the lowest price at which you're prepared to sell.

At Market: when you tell your stockbroker that you're prepared to buy or sell at whatever the market price is.

Bear: a person who expects prices to fall and sells shares hoping to make a profit by buying them again later at a lower price. If they're wrong and prices rise, they make a loss instead of a profit.

Bear Market: a falling market, where a 'bear' claws market prices down.

Blue Chip Stock: shares in a company with a good reputation for making profits in good times or bad. Share prices are higher and generally more stable long-term but dividends are usually low.

Bond: a loan you make to a government (or semi-government) body for a fixed term at a fixed rate of interest. The government guarantees to pay you back.

Bonus Issue: when bonus or free shares are given to existing shareholders, in a set ratio—eg. one for ten means one bonus share for every ten shares you hold on a set date.

Books Closing Date: the date a company chooses to 'close its books' so they can figure out who gets paid dividends, bonus issues, new issues etc. on a set date—even if you've only owned their shares for a day!

Brokerage Fee: the amount charged by a stockbroker for buying or selling your shares on your behalf. Standard fees for a full service broker are often 2.5% of the value of the shares bought or sold, with a minimum payment of $50. Since $50 is also 2.5% of $2000, it's cost-effective to keep your buy and sell orders above $2000 when dealing with a full service broker. Internet brokerage fees are cheaper—usually $10 to $30 for trades up to $10,000. *Caution:* Internet brokers sometimes restrict you to buying 'at market'.

Bull Market: a rising market, where an imaginary 'bull' tosses market prices up.

C.H.E.S.S. (Clearing House Electronic Subregister System): one statement is issued for each company that you own shares in as proof. Statements are sent out whenever there's a change in the number you own.

Dividend: a payment made usually twice a year to distribute part of a company's net profit to shareholders as a reward for investing in the company.

Earnings Per Share (EPS): the company's net profit divided by the total number of shares in the company and expressed as cents per share. It's another good indicator for investors choosing which shares to buy or sell.

Float: also known as an Initial Public Offer (IPO) this refers to the money raised for a company by selling shares to the public. A company 'floats' on the stockmarket only after it has fulfilled all ASX Listing Rules—which are stricter than just the rules under Corporations Law.

Green Chip Shares: shares in a growing company which is really starting to perform. Green chips are usually cheaper than blue chips, and tend to experience more regular or greater price fluctuations or 'cycles'. Most of the companies that make your shortlist will be green chips; however, such green chips can and have grown to become blue chips.

Net Asset Backing (NAB, also known as Asset Backing): an important check for investors! NAB is where net assets of a company in dollars are divided by the total number of shares issued. For example, if *Thingy Inc* has $100,000 in net assets and 10,000 shares issued, then it has a Net Asset Backing of $10.00 per share. Compare the NAB to the company's earning capacity and share price to see if you're onto a good deal.

Net Tangible Assets (NTA): slightly different to NAB, it's the net assets owned by shareholders of a company.

Price/Earnings Ratio (P/E ratio): the market price of a share, divided by the company's earnings per share. As a general rule, the P/E ratio is a handy indicator for beginners because it tells you how the big investors expect a company to perform. A low P/E ratio indicates that most sharemarket traders think the company will have a poorer performance than its competitors with higher P/E ratios. A high P/E ratio however, can mean either that the company is expected to do well, or that it is being valued on a good asset backing.

Stockbroker: a licensed member of the Australian Stock Exchange who buys and sells stocks, shares and other securities for their clients. Not all stockbrokers will deal with small investors. You can also buy and sell online through virtual brokers, but make sure you know if they deal at market, at discretion, or at limit before committing yourself to an order.

T+3: this means Trade Date plus 3, meaning you've got three business days to pay up after the day you buy your shares. It also means you get paid about three business days after your shares were bought by someone else.

Yield: this is the effective return to investors from a particular security, expressed as a percentage of the current market price. So shares selling at $2 each may be reported to give a 10% dividend, but if the price rises to $4 each by the time you buy them—and if the dividend remains the same as last time—your dividend yield will only be 5%. This works in reverse too.

Appendix IX

Notes Pages

Use this appendix to record your notes or jot down any reminders for things you wish to research later.